AN UNCONVENTIONAL JOURNEY INTO LEADERSHIP

MATT GARMAN

To Ben,

With Ugly Best
Wishes

An Unconventional Journey into Leadership

ISBN: 978-1-8383299-9-0

Published by **Matt Garman 2024**
London, England UK

Author: Matt Garman
Writer: Kerry Parkinson Day
Front Cover Photography: Liz Marie Jay
Rear Cover Photography: World's Toughest Row – Ben Duffy/Penny Bird
Cover Design: Klassic Designs

ACKNOWLEDGMENTS

Thinking back over the years there are so many people who've inspired me, challenged me, taught me, shown me the path I wanted to travel and the path I definitely didn't want to follow. One of my reasons in writing this book was so that I could pay tribute to those people and to tell them what a privilege it is to count them as my friends.

My wife, Sam, is of course top of the list. She is an inspiration to me, the heart of our family and although she hates my mad adventures, she understands and always supports me with such good grace. I know how lucky I am to have such a person to love and who loves me too.

My wonderful children, Joseph and Mollie. They are my happy place, my motivation and inspiration, and I'm so proud of who they are; I'm prouder of them than anything else in my life.

My Dad, who I loved and came to know and better understand more fully later in my life.

My Mum, who I love. I hope she is proud of who I have become.

My brothers, Jonathan and David, without whom my growing up would have been incredibly boring and who continue to hold me to account even to this day.

My Uncle John, my first real mentor, who showed me how to catch bass, respect the environment and that I didn't have to wear a suit to earn a living.

Buzz, my school buddy, early business partner, lifelong friend and always the voice of reason.

Andy, my school buddy, lifelong friend, godfather to Joseph and someone I've always looked up to.

My friend, Jason, YTS buddy, fishing friend and early influence in getting me to know when I'm being an idiot.

Brian (BC), business associate initially who then became a teammate in our attempt to swim the English Channel, and a wonderful sounding board.

Sandra, swim buddy and pocket dynamo who separates the girls from the boys.

David (Coxy), training partner, swim teammate, family friend and simply incredible guy.

Neil (Diesel), fellow rugby club player, friend and all-round amazing human being who was our anchor and engine who showed us how to row an Ocean.

Steve 'Woolley', friend and all-round incredible teammate who willingly took on the domestic tasks to keep us all fed and watered and rowed his heart out to get us home.

CONTENTS

PREFACE

I had an idyllic early childhood. I was the middle of three brothers and we lived near Harbury, Warwickshire. I never worried about much. We went to school and longed for weekends and holidays when we could roam around the countryside near our house. We played in the fields, walked for miles and climbed trees, only going home when we were hungry.

When I was 8 years old, I took part in a sponsored walk. It wasn't a fixed length so I just kept going and going until I'd walked 26 miles. I don't remember being tired and I probably wasn't because we were used to walking or running everywhere, all day. We were always outdoors.

Everything changed when Dad got a better job and we moved to Seaford. Seaford is a town on the East Sussex coast and our lives changed overnight. I was 11. My older brother started at Seaford Head Secondary School, and my younger brother and I were sent to the Catholic primary school because it was the only one with space for us mid-year. I mention this because suddenly we had moved away from everything I'd known and loved, which felt like leaving my life behind, a life where I knew my place. The countryside was our playground, and we knew it, it was safe, it was a perfect fit. Then, after arriving in Seaford, one of the things I loved most in life was brutally taken away: rugby. First, at school, they only played football, and the local rugby club trained on Sunday mornings. My Dad wouldn't let me play on Sundays.

I can't say for sure, but it seems to me that all these changes happening at a young age led to my lifelong feeling of not quite knowing where I fit in. I know I'm not alone in these feelings, many of us have them, and I know I've had a lucky and privileged life, which I'm thankful for. I also know that anxiety and a feeling of displacement have always affected me, influenced my decisions and I still feel I must prove myself in everything I do.

And so to the Atlantic Row. This is by far the most life challenging, life-changing adventure I've experienced so far. Am I closer to being confident in my leadership ability and knowing where I fit in? Conquering those feelings of anxiety and imposter syndrome? The simple answer is no.

That said, I am closer to understanding I might never overcome them, and perhaps that doesn't even matter. What is important is what I learn along the journey, and what I share to help others who may also struggle. My purpose is clear; keep learning, keep sharing and only measure myself against who I was yesterday, to make sure I keep working to be the best person I can be.

I've always liked that old saying: A fool learns by their own mistakes, a wise person learns from the mistakes of others.

I wrote this book for the wise, for those who might learn from some of the mistakes I've made, and to share the valuable lessons of leadership that I've learned and continue to learn every day.

Matt Garman
Seaford, 2024

CHAPTER 1
MY DAD

For most of my adult years, Dad and I weren't on the same wavelength. When he was diagnosed with terminal prostate cancer, I felt completely helpless. I thought about all that lost time. I had been angry for so long and didn't even know why, but now that he'd become a little less independent and we'd grown closer, the desire to make him proud was stronger than ever.

It was hard watching a man who'd been very active, strong, and powerful, emotionally as well as physically, become less steady on his feet until the day came I had to physically carry him to my car to take him to look out at the sea.

He was fragile and it frustrated him, knowing that it was only going to get worse. It was a typical windy day with a chill in the air and we were quiet as we watched the waves. Not knowing how to talk to my dying Dad. My thoughts were all over the place trying not to think too far into the future and yet, in the back of my mind, I was planning a very real adventure that would take years of preparation, years my Dad didn't have.

Suddenly, I blurted out, "Dad, I'm thinking of rowing across the Atlantic Ocean."

He sat very still, looking out to sea, the silence was heavy. And then he turned to me, that twinkle of delight in his eye, a huge grin on his face, and he said with a chuckle, "Of course, you are, why doesn't that surprise me?"

In this grin, with these words, I felt loved, but more than that, I felt I had found the place I wanted to be, a place where I had the confidence to try anything, because my Dad believed in me, and I knew my Dad loved me.

OUR FINAL DAY OF ROWING IN 'THE WORLD'S TOUGHEST ROW'

Log: Day 49. 04:30

It's early morning, still dark outside, but this should be our last day. We have under 50 miles to go. Yesterday we were all feeling very emotional because we're in sight of the finish line and are all so desperate to finish what has been a very long seven weeks of relentless hard work, physical endurance and sleep deprivation. We've long since run out of tea, coffee, biscuits and chocolate. We had a team talk and all agreed to crack on and reach Antigua today. We know we'll be pushing ourselves really hard to make it, but this is it.

Now we're on the final approach and although it's been a very long and hard 48 hours, it's been fantastic. We were all complaining about how sweaty and dirty we were and how we needed to make sure we didn't stink, but then the heavens opened and we had torrential rain. What a gift! We got out the soap, stripped off and 'showered' in the rain. Luckily, we are still far enough out there's no danger of anyone taking happy snaps of us in the buff. We spent some time chatting and listening to music and then we watched the perfect sunset. The three of us alone as the darkness of the Atlantic landscape covered us for the final time. After that it was on with the preparation for our arrival, our head torches blinding us as we worked to bring the boat safely home.

Leadership Wisdom

Leadership often requires the strength to manage self-doubt in critical moments to safeguard the team.

Ian Couch, the Chief Safety Officer, had told us to stay as close to land as possible. As Neil and Steve rowed slowly and strongly around Shirley Heights, now in perfect unison, I was hand steering while full of anxiety. Did Ian mean for us to be quite this close? We could hear the water lapping on the cliffs, and it felt like we would run aground any moment. It would be on me if I had made such a terrible mistake in these last hours. Neil and Woolley trusted me to bring us home. If they had no doubt then why couldn't I feel the same confidence? We had a 15-knot following wind and I kept jumping in and out of the cabin checking the GPS to ensure we were exactly where we should be. And then, suddenly, we rounded a final piece of headland and the wind stopped completely. The water was calm and we were ready for the final approach formalities.

A rib came out to collect our passports, the media boat joined us and we followed it into the inlet. We couldn't make out the distant red lights and thought they must be some kind of construction. We'd become so accustomed to the vast emptiness of the Atlantic that we required time to understand what we were seeing. And then there was an incredible noise and we realised the red lights were the masts of superyachts moored in the harbour as they pressed their horns to welcome us home. The horns seemed to split the air, the loudest sound we'd heard in seven weeks.

Leadership Wisdom

A good leader will recognise the contribution of every person involved in a successful outcome, even if they're not in the team.

As is the custom for every boat that finishes, we lit our flares and roared as we neared the jetty. The emotion, the adrenaline, made us feel like giants, and it seemed impossible that we were here. We had done it! Our families were just moments away and as skipper, I had promised myself and my teammates that I would not step off the boat until they were safely back on dry land, that I would be the last to leave the boat. I waited for Neil and Steve to alight and when they were safely on the jetty, I left the boat. We all stumbled, our sea legs after seven weeks at sea making the concrete pontoon feel like it was floating.

The first person I sought out was Ian Couch. For 49 days, our lives had literally been in his hands, and it was very important to me to thank him. Then there were a few formalities before we could finally reunite with our families waiting anxiously. I fell into the arms of my wife, son and daughter, and didn't want to let go. It had been such a long and emotional seven weeks that I didn't want these moments to end. I was home at last.

CHAPTER 2
INTRODUCTION TO THE IDEA OF LEADERSHIP

L eading a team is what I like best. I have achieved significantly challenging events by myself but once I'd crossed the finish line, they'd all felt pretty meaningless. I missed the teamwork, sharing the crazy stuff, hard training sessions, celebrating with teammates and the lasting fellowship of a joint venture.

My first experience of leadership was with my brothers. I'm the middle of three, and my older brother naturally assumed the status as our leader. We didn't even think about it, he was the oldest and it was the natural order of things. We would have followed him anywhere.

As I got older, I accepted that whoever led us; the rugby captain, the coach, a teacher, my Dad, had all got something that I didn't have. Then, as the years piled on, I started to understand that while someone might be a designated leader because of their age, position or job, they might not be any good at it. This was a very exciting idea to me because I already felt I was a natural leader.

I don't think there's any right or wrong way to go about the business of leadership. It can be complex, rewarding, thankless, frustrating, and impossible, but when your team starts to be consistently successful, and you realise that you're no longer flying by the seat of your pants, you can start to enjoy it. I think enjoying being a leader really matters because confidence and enjoyment are contagious. I know I'm most successful when I see my team enjoying the challenges we face together, and overcoming them together.

I am confident in my ability to lead, but I never lose sight of my goals: to be better, to keep learning and to keep improving.

MOVING DOWN SOUTH

When we moved from the Midlands to the South Coast my horizons broadened and while I had less access to outdoor freedom, and I was not allowed to play rugby on Sundays, there was the sea and my Uncle John.

Leadership Wisdom

Show your team how to do something and then trust them to do it themselves.

John Darling, Uncle John, was my first mentor. He introduced me to fishing and the joys of the wonderful countryside where we lived. He was an accomplished and published author, photographer and leader in his field. His example of being able to earn a living while not wearing a suit and tie was life changing for me, it opened up a world of possibilities. He was completely comfortable in his own skin. He taught me how to cast a line and catch fish. We would walk down from Seaford Head to Cuckmere Haven, he put a rod in my hand and after a few basic tips expected me to feel my way and learn fishing by watching him.

Actually, doing it myself, being trusted to do it, was perhaps my first glimpse of good leadership.

At school, while I was reported to be sharp and bright, I was already unable or perhaps unwilling to focus long enough on subjects I didn't like, to do well. I was always in the middle of the middle streams. If I'd studied hard, as was suggested at every parent teacher interview, I could have done really well. I just didn't see the point.

My family embraced academia as the only yard stick by which we were judged. My Dad was a Consulting Engineer, my Mum was a high-level music teacher, my older brother is a Doctor of Mathematics, and my younger brother is a Doctor of Horti-culture.

Me? I've got one O' level and for far too long, felt like a failure.

LEAVING SCHOOL, THE JOURNEY BEGINS

Having rejected my family values, formal education, University, qualifications and set career path, though feeling I was making the right choice for myself, I clung to the example of Uncle John and, at the tender age of 16, rushed headlong into adulthood. I left school and joined the Youth Training Scheme, taking a six-week residential course for commercial fishing. There, I learned to read a chart and compass, sea survival, basic firefighting and first aid.

In this new environment, with a mix of others from different backgrounds, I realised I was finding what they were teaching easy and I was astonished at how some others on the course were having difficulty keeping up.

During the last week of the course in the sea survival unit, we had to go to a lake, get in a life raft, capsize it and then right it again. It was a typical winter, cold, rainy and dismal. Righting a life raft when you're 16, freezing, soaking wet and miserable is bloody hard. We'd arrived on a bus, and I quickly realised we'd all be on the riverbank until the last person had completed the exercise successfully. That meant once you'd had your turn, you shivered, wet, cold and miserable, until everyone had finished. Normally, I like to go first and attack a task full-on, leading the way, but on this particularly cold morning, I knew the smarter thing to do would be to make sure I was picked last in the group, so that my time waiting wet and tired in the freezing cold would be reduced, and would lessen the misery of the exercise. At least, going last, I could dry and warm myself quicker. I was amazed that nobody else figured this out, and I think for the first time I understood that being smart wasn't only connected to book learning and doing well in school. Because of this, I felt a new confidence in myself. In the real world, it didn't matter that I hadn't done well at school. I knew it wasn't because I was stupid, I simply wasn't interested in what they were teaching.

Presented with something I wanted to learn in a hands-on environment, I found easy. I was able to grasp concepts and understand complex instructions with ease. I know now it's because I'm a visual and kinaesthetic learner and my brain doesn't respond to limited listen/learn situations. Back when I was at school there was less variety and opportunity to match learning to teaching methods. If you didn't fit the standard, narrow teaching mould, you were often labelled stupid or difficult.

Nearly forty years later when I was training to row the Atlantic, all those early safety lessons for life at sea came back to me like I'd learned them yesterday.

CHAPTER 3
WORKING ON THE FISHING TRAWLER

At the end of the course, we were all allocated a place on a commercial trawler. Unfortunately, my first placement didn't go ahead because there was an incident on the boat I was due to join.

It was a boat based out of Shoreham, along the coast not far from Seaford, and stayed at sea for a week at a time. The boat was 90 feet long and the week before my placement, it had caught an unexploded wartime mine in its nets. This mine detonated with the hauling movement and blew the back of the boat out of the water. Close to sinking as it took on water, the boat had to be towed back to the harbour.

My YTS (Youth Training Scheme) placement was hurriedly updated and instead I was sent to join a day boat that worked out of Newhaven. This suited me much better because it was so close to home.

Unfortunately for me, leaving school also meant leaving home, as my parents didn't approve of my life choices, but I was already on a path that would see me learning by jumping in with both feet, taking risks and making mistakes.

Leadership Wisdom

Clarity of purpose, understanding the rules.

I had absolutely no idea what I was good at and even at that early stage, I didn't think it was going to be my long-term future, but it was the start of the adventure.

There was a lot to like at first. I was living out of home, making my own decisions and earning money, even if only a pitiful weekly YTS allowance together with a £20 bonus from the skipper on top if I'd worked hard. Admittedly, I was living in a terrible rented room about 3m x 3m, sharing a bathroom that had seen cleaner days, and living on takeaway food and toast.

Life at sea was hard but varied, and there I learned some of my most important leadership lessons. Clarity of purpose, preparation and understanding my role, the rules and the importance of teamwork. I didn't really have much of a social life and spent very little money because my life was working, working and more working.

In that first year my weekly YTS allowance was £27.30, in my second year it increased to the grand total of £35, although the skipper gave me a £20 bonus, which made it a little more liveable and he didn't need to do that.

I remember one week in my first year when the fish were so plentiful that every time we went out we doubled and trebled our usual catch. As luck would have it, I was alone with the skipper as our other crew member had gone for a week's holiday to the West Country. I worked my heart out, hauling the nets in, gutting fish, completing three or four times my usual workload just to get the job done. Our absent crew member heard about our huge catches and returned early because, knowing his share for these two unusual days would be worth more than a normal week's pay, he couldn't afford to miss out, because he knew his share for two days would be more than his pay for a normal week.

Leadership Wisdom

Reward hard work and recognise the value of workers who go above and beyond expectations.

At last, the hard graft of the week finished, and our Friday payday came. The skipper congratulated me, said how much he appreciated my efforts and handed over my YTS money. I knew he'd given the other crewman a few hundred pounds for the two days he'd worked, so I had great expectations. After all, I'd done the bulk of the work every day, so when he solemnly handed over my usual twenty-pound note, I was shattered. 20 quid! I calculated I'd worked a seven-day week, averaging 16 hours a day. That's over a hundred solid hours hauling nets, gutting, washing and boxing fish. I was expecting at least £100 and felt as gutted as the fish. That day, however, I learned a very valuable and a very tough lesson about leadership.

Income for the crew was based on a share of the catch, which was variable and based on trust. The skipper paid everyone in cash at the end of every week and so the crew lived for those good catches that would boost their income.

The crew's share of the catch was based on percentage. After expenses were accounted for, the owner took half and then the remainder was shared out with the skipper receiving 5/9ths, the crewman taking 4/9ths. I was promised that if I stuck it out until after my YTS two years, they would reduce their share slightly and I would get a total of 1/9th of the wages.

After my two years YTS, I stayed on the boat and my earnings went up and down according to our catch. My wages were a mixed bag, pretty good or really bad. I couldn't rely on a regular income because I never knew what it was going to be.

However, with the early starts, irregular hours and saving every penny I earned, I didn't have much of a social life and saved every penny I could. I was paid a lot in cash, which I put in a supermarket carrier bag that was stuffed under my bed because I could never make it to the bank when it was open.

After five years, I had saved enough for a deposit on a flat. On the day of completion I took my carrier bag full of cash to the solicitor who got his PA to count it out on the desk. I also took him a box of freshly caught fish and a lobster as a thank you. Looking back, I can only imagine the story he might've told his friends, but I was too young and naïve to think about it. Having bought my first flat, I was so full of hope. I was 19 and mortgage interest rates stood at 14.25%. Life got way too serious way too soon.

Now that I had a mortgage to pay, I became more anxious about earning good, regular money. It was vital. Relying on a very low wage with the hope of a cash bonus after a good catch was too risky.

Leadership Wisdom

Reward, recognition and meeting expectations builds strong teams that thrive on success.

I had learned a lot about life in my years on the trawler. One of those hard-learned lessons was that expectation rarely meets reality. As the years passed, and I was no longer on the Youth Training Scheme but a proper part of the crew earning a living by being reliant on what we caught.

Leadership Wisdom

Always pay what you owe promptly, especially to your team.

I didn't realise it at the time, but I had started to understand more about leadership than I realised. One thing that stood out, which to this day I still adhere to, is a lesson about one of the most emotive subjects in life - money.

Specifically, the importance of paying what you have committed to, without question or delay. Every Friday was pay day, the best day of the week, and one of my clearest memories of those days was being paid on time, with the skipper and owner checking, double-checking and reconciling to the penny.

My anxiety was rising about my future and although I'd always been aware of the power of the sea, and the dangers of working on a fishing trawler, they ramped up astronomically when I witnessed a burial at sea. It was for a young guy who worked on a boat that tied up next to us. He had young children and was killed during an accident on deck.

It suddenly became so real how quickly life can be snatched away and what a precious gift it is. I could see clearly that I was wasting mine and that it was time to grow up, quit fishing and get serious.

But if this wasn't my calling, where did I fit in?

CHAPTER 4
LOSING MY SEA LEGS, GAINING A PURPOSE

My life needed an overhaul. Still only a few years out of school with no career plans, and only my fishing boat experience to recommend me to potential employers, I didn't feel like I had much to offer. I'd picked up some valuable lessons about leadership, which I still employ to this day, but as the lowest rung on the boat, I'd had no opportunity to exercise them, and of course had zero credibility. No sensible employer would have taken a chance on who I was then, no matter how I might have blagged my way through an interview.

For me, the most valuable thing about school was the group of close friends I'd made, lifelong friends who taught me about love and loyalty, and not always thinking about yourself first. And as has often been the case in my life, it is friends who've shown their belief in me and helped me take the next step.

Becoming increasingly anxious about no money coming in and no job prospects, I was drowning my sorrows in the pub with a mate who was working as a milkman and wasn't happy either. He was moaning about how the rounds had all recently been franchised, which meant he was responsible for all of the debts and was unable to take any holiday because there was nobody to provide cover for him.

Over a few drinks and a lot of swearing about how unfair life was, a great idea was born. I could set myself up as a relief milkman, I would cover not only my mate's round when he wanted time off, but everyone else's too. I wouldn't have my own round, but I'd pretty much have full time work covering all the rounds.

As I always do, I charged headlong into the work, giving it my all. It seemed easy enough, stick to the round, ignore the fact that I could run faster than the electric float could travel, and get the round done, the milk delivered as quickly as possible.

I stuck at it for eighteen months before realising it, too, was a dead-end job, not a career, and I got fed up collecting the money from people who half the time pretended to be out because they couldn't pay. I was getting depressed most days, the constant struggle, feeling like I was locked into something that wasn't getting me where I wanted to go.

I used to run the rounds to try and get them finished quicker. One day, whilst running too fast, and carrying too many bottles of milk, I slipped down some steps and my left hand went through the bottles that I had been carrying as they smashed.

Leadership Wisdom

Set goals that align with your vision. Don't be afraid to adjust them as you progress towards the future you want.

I knocked on the door of the customer and he gave me a tea towel to wrap my hand and called an ambulance. I had pieces of glass stuck in my hand and I knew it was bad. On the way to the hospital, I wondered if I'd ever be able to use my hand again.

Once again, it was time to think about the future. Financially, I was going backwards and the mortgage was a constant worry. Life felt too risky with not enough money, no direction and not knowing what, if anything, I was good at.

I wanted an unconventional path; I just didn't know how to go about it. How do you find the thing you're good at?

Now I would tell my younger self to try everything that comes your way. Seek out opportunities and keep on trying until you find what works. At about this time I went to a franchise exhibition in London; I couldn't afford the ticket, but somehow managed to talk my way inside. I'd seen an ad and thought (naively) that I could find a business to run, though I hadn't quite realised how much money I would need to even think about starting a franchise. Afterwards, I was disheartened and still hadn't got a clue what to do.

The setbacks I'd already experienced had hardened my ambition and given me more purpose. I wanted to earn more money, have control of my destiny, do something that I could be proud of and not put myself in physical danger. These were the key things I was looking for. I also wanted to be respected and do something worthwhile. I started learning what that might be by really looking at the world around me and eliminating anything that wouldn't meet these goals. I had begun to act a little more seriously about establishing a proper career.

Soon after, I got mailshotted by a life insurance business: 'Run your own business without the overheads'. This was the only thing that came out of going to the franchise exhibition. Selling insurance wasn't something I could see myself doing, but it did tick the boxes on my must have list, and the company offered six weeks sales training. Sales hadn't been on my radar of possibilities, but the training sounded like a good idea. And, how hard could it be?

Selling insurance? I could do that!

Leadership Wisdom

Match your leadership to your team.

The training was pretty much selling skills, and very unlike my school experience. I ran with it, passing each module easily. If school had been taught this way using early computers, a little like basic video games, I could've sailed through it.

I can't say I liked insurance, but the training woke up something deep inside me, a little kernel of knowledge that I had a lot of natural selling ability. It all seemed so logical, the training came so easily, I got it immediately and realised that I already had a huge appetite for everything business related; talking to people, working with them, finding solutions, and I couldn't wait to get started.

Once the training was finished, we were sent out to sell on a commission-only basis. The money was up and down, and I hadn't realised that a sale wasn't a sale until after the three months grace period was finished. A large percentage of people drop out before that, and the commission is forfeit. This meant a time lag between working and being paid, and I never knew how much I would actually earn.

The uncertainty meant I couldn't afford to pay the mortgage and eat, and I ended up totally skint. My anxiety skyrocketed; I was surviving on plain pasta with a squirt of ketchup and the occasional army ration pack that my pal Andy shared with me when he came to visit when on leave. I made the only decision I could, I rented out my flat to pay the mortgage and moved into a small room at Andy's Mum's house.

It was really tough swallowing my pride, but it was better than losing my flat, which was my first step to the life I knew I wanted. I had realised that, while I liked selling and was really good at it, I hated life insurance.

Leadership Wisdom

If a person loves their work, offer them the opportunity to do more.

Again, at crisis point, a lifesaving conversation with a friend created a new opportunity. My great friend, Buzz, said his boss, Mel, was looking for a salesperson. He talked me up, and I was so desperate for the job that I said I'd work commission only if he took me on. I asked him to forward me £500 a month, which I would pay back out of my commission when I made sales. I was very confident I could do it. I had the arrogance of youth, the desperation of a person looking for a better life and the confidence of someone determined to change their experiences, both good and bad, into a valuable asset.

My plan was to sell IT during the day and life insurance in the evening. This lasted two days. The new IT sales job hooked me. I loved it and I couldn't wait step away from the door to door selling of life insurance. I learned like a crazy man on a mission, loving every minute of a more relaxed lifestyle, and only had to work five days a week now.

My guaranteed £500 per month was a godsend, and it took me a good six months to build a solid sales pipeline. During this critical time, I broke my leg badly and could barely walk, let alone drive to see customers. This was long before online meetings were a normal way of doing business. A friend had contacted me and asked if I could make up the numbers for their football team as they were a player short. Although football is not a game I've played much, or even particularly like, I agreed to help out so they didn't have to forfeit the game. I came on for the last five minutes of the match. In wanting to make an impression, I went flat out into a tackle and my leg snapped. I was stretchered off and spent months in a cast. Needing to get back to work, I would make phone calls with my leg propped on a chair and when I had meetings with customers, Mel or one of the other guys would drive me to them.

Leadership Wisdom

Learn to see beyond the immediate picture, support your team and help them reach their potential.

Mel was an astute guy and a genuinely good person. He could already see the difference I was making and that the work I was putting in would yield good results. Broken leg notwithstanding, Mel's faith was repaid, and my confidence soared when, after nine months of presenting, probing and nurturing prospects, my hard work started to pay off big time. The orders started to flow in and I was earning more than five thousand in commission every month. I didn't look back.

I was so good at this and couldn't stop selling, I had a thirst for it. For the first time in my life, I wanted to learn more, became studious about sales, and started reading and listening to other more experienced people. Again, I thought of school and how easy it must be for kids who liked what they were being taught. Now I was keen because I could see a reason for the knowledge. I knew if I learnt more, I could earn more. I also started to notice how much good or bad leadership affected the way people behaved at work and in life. So, I studied more, gained experience and found new and better ways of doing things.

Leadership Wisdom

If you're naturally good at something, more training and more practice makes you even better.

I reflected on all the different leaders I'd had in my life. The rugby coaches, Dad, teachers and the skipper on the boat. I started to understand exactly when the things they did resonated with me, and those who left me cold and sometimes angry and resentful.

By the time I was 30, I was earning great money, I was a star salesperson, and started to see how the business could be improved and exactly what was holding us back. I was great at my job and my ambition was overwhelming. After work one night, I was having a conversation with Mel, the Managing Director. I laid out exactly what I thought needed to be done, pointing out his failure without any regard for how he might take it. It was a small IT business selling hardware and accounting software. Mel owned the business but had already sold 15% in shares, costing £5000, to me, Buzz and one other longstanding member of staff. Mel was still the majority shareholder, though, and all the main decisions were his.

I was looking to the future, had always felt the hardware side of the business had limited scope and so I suggested that the software side had more potential for real growth. He looked me straight in the eye and said, "well, if you think you can do any better, why don't you run the fucking company!"

I said I'd love to, but not with only a minority share.

He followed up with, "OK, if you want the majority share you can buy it from me for £150,000. We'll swap shares, you'll have my majority share, I'll have your 15% and you can get on and run it." It was almost conversational rather than a major business transaction.

We locked eyes, we agreed, shook hands and I said, 'Done!"

15 minutes later I was on my way home, late, having agreed to buy a business. What the hell had I just done?

To put it in perspective, at that time, Sam and I had just bought our first house for £92,500, we were mortgaged up to the hilt and had no more savings. On the spur of the moment, I had spent money we didn't have without consulting my wife, and now I had to work out how to finance it. Quite apart from that, we didn't have children yet and I hadn't given any thought to how this would affect our plans to start a family.

I assumed control the following January and things changed immediately. I was left with some IT engineers running an IT department that generated roughly two-thirds of the company's revenue, the other third came from the sale of accounting software. In those long, distant days (25 years ago!), during the relatively early stages of PC networks, most PC and server repairs had to be done onsite. Many of the engineers who serviced our clients were a law unto themselves and inside of that group sat the other 15% shareholder of the company.

The turnover at that point was a little over £1million per annum, but there was no clear vision. When I did the deal to take it over the company, my 30-year-old self didn't restart the company but instead, I continued operating as it was. I tried very hard to keep everyone onside and it didn't really hit me how huge a step I'd taken in a very short space of time, from commission-only sales-person to Managing Director. Almost from the start, I was over-whelmed by everything I didn't know. I knew nothing about leadership, I was good at sales and had an aptitude for business, but leadership training? I didn't even know what I didn't know. It was an almost too steep a learning curve and it very nearly sank me.

CHAPTER 5
LEADERSHIP 101

I thought I knew business. I had bought the company because I thought I could run it better. I didn't quite realise, because I'd never done it before, that business leaders are under constant pressure to lead by example, motivate their staff, report up, if there's a Board, Partners or Investors, cascade down, exceed targets and create effective growth strategies.

Leadership Wisdom

Encourage people to try what they have learned/know and don't criticise them for taking time to build their confidence.

To fulfil all these requirements, a leader needs an incredibly diverse range of skills. Not many people have the full set of strategic, diplomatic, business acumen and people skills, and I didn't even know I needed to have them.

Leaders may have one or more of these attributes, but often a person is promoted because they're good at what they're currently doing but that doesn't necessarily mean they'd be good at leading others too. In my case, this was true.

I was so good at my job that it put me in the position to buy the company. I had experience in sports leadership and I just assumed those skills would easily transfer. More than that, I expected my new position as Managing Director, along with my own stellar performance record would be enough to enable me to lead. It quickly dawned on me that my new title and sales skills were not significant, they were only the tip of a huge iceberg of what I needed to make the company a success.

Over the years since, I have been called in to help many companies fix problems arising from promoting people who've been pumped to land a leadership role. Often, they revel in the fact that they've been recognised, rewarded and then forget their new job is big a step up and requires different skills. It's vital to understand that a promotion to lead a team isn't the end of the journey to success, it's just the beginning of the next journey. Everything that came before was simple compared to what's to come.

Being good at what you do and focussing on achieving your own goals and targets, even if you're part of team, allows you to be selfish. You're primarily responsible for yourself and your target. Of course, you answer to your manager, but your primary focus is on what *you* individually need to do for success.

To lead a team, or head up a company as I did, often requires an entirely different skill. When you face the team for the first time, they'll expect you to have all the answers and if you're a first-time leader, it's very likely you won't have those answers. Yet.

Although there is no substitute for experience, there are a few things that make a transition to leadership easier. I learnt this the hard way whilst riding the huge learning curve and trying not to make fatal mistakes.

CONSISTENCY

I learned early that success isn't only about your knowledge or position. It's very important to be consistent in your leadership. This means all elements of leadership, from practical arrangements to the more difficult areas such as being able to control your frustrations at minor (or major) mistakes, and not favouring team members who share your interests. Emotional intelligence, empathy and considerate behaviour are just as important as motivation and practical training.

PERSONAL GROWTH

It's tempting to relax a bit when you attain your leadership goal. The team must follow you, it's in their contract and you're their acknowledged leader. But really, the journey has just begun. Your team are now looking for you to motivate, protect and propel them to success. They must learn that they can't sit back and leave it all to you. You have to know when to get out of their way and let them grow. You also have to continue your own personal growth and widen your knowledge if you're going to continue leading by example.

INFLUENCE

Any good leader worth their title should be able to influence their team to ensure their success. Find out what the team need to do, how they need to approach their work, what tools they need to achieve success and make sure they are trained and ready. Make it simple by encouraging open communication. Don't be afraid to hear what they have to say and don't be afraid to influence their behaviour. Their success is your success.

VISION

I talk a lot about vision because it's so important, though ultimately vision is just clarity about where you're going, your end game and how you intend to get there. Be very clear to your team about your vision. Define what success looks like and make sure your team knows it, understands it and is on board with it.

CONTROL YOUR OWN DESTINY

I know I have control issues; a lot of leaders do. When I feel under pressure, I know I tend to revert to micro-management, which is not conducive to strong leadership. It simply sends the message that you have minimal confidence in the ability of your team. To control your own destiny, you need to have the courage to face issues and challenges without being afraid to ask for input from your team. The best teams are those that feel valued for their contribution. Invite your team to solve problems and encourage original and innovative ideas. Building others up does not diminish you, quite the opposite, in fact, as it shows you're a confident and generous leader, and this in itself will inspire respect.

LEADING WITH A LIGHT HAND

Never hamper the natural ability of your people by nit-picking and micro-management. A leader with a light hand is the one you trust because they build your confidence by believing in you and showing by their actions that they know you are capable and equipped to rise to any occasion. And always remember that innovation should be encouraged because continuous improvement is how best practice stays best practice. The best ideas usually come from those at the sharp end, whose day-to-day work drives the company.

REGULAR TRAINING

One of the key roles of good leadership is to train, or organise regular training, for the team. Each person must know what to do, how to do it and how to fit into the unique culture of a company. This doesn't end with good onboarding. Just like a sports team, set pieces, ways of communicating with customers and other areas of the business need to be trained for and practiced regularly. Introducing a dynamic and sustainable system of what works for your company is vital to ensure each team is in the best place to win business and meet their targets. We understand why sports teams practice each week and train for specific on pitch scenarios with specialist coaches. To put this in context, a rugby team trains for 5 full days to play for 80 minutes. Why do so many businesses think that training and practice is not necessary for their teams?

MEMORY

Never forget how you felt when you were in their position within the team. What type of leader did you respond to best?

Make a point of analysing all your interactions with past managers, good and bad, what resonated and inspired you, and what made you want to pull the covers over your head and not go to work? It's likely that these things affect your team members in exactly the same way. If you're in doubt, ask for feedback from your team. It can be confronting, but it's also a quick way to build trust and become a better leader.

COURAGE

I've mentioned courage before and it's because I think it takes courage to be a leader. You are sticking your head above the parapet and saying 'I can do this'. One of the hardest things I have learned during my leadership journey is that you can't put off difficult conversations and tough decisions. They are so much tougher if you just wait, hoping they will somehow resolve themselves without having to do anything. Take it from me, they won't.

I think it's the part of leadership that's most difficult and most confronting because it is the end of the line scenario, often involving one or more team members. After considering all the options early regarding the matter, sought advice and made sure you've done absolutely all you can do, make the decision. This applies to every decision, but most especially the tough ones. Dealing with a situation in a timely way will be the best outcome for everyone involved whatever situation you're dealing with. It takes courage and it's a good reminder that leadership is never about being the most popular member of the team.

COMMUNICATION

Good communication is vital for success. Learn how to communicate best with all your key stakeholders; your team, peers, investment partners, your Board and your customers. It may seem like spinning plates, but good communication is the key to leadership and success. Keeping everyone appraised of how things are going, any issues and great results, means you'll never be put on the spot and have to defend what you're doing. If there's an issue that you don't want to share, think about how the alarm bells might sound. It will likely be found out, possibly when it's much harder to fix. Raise it immediately, ask for help, get it sorted quickly and cleanly. I can't begin to emphasise the importance of good and open communication. Secrets poison a team, harm a business and hamper success. Good leaders build trust and confidence by setting clear expectations with timely and authentic communication.

TIME TO RELAX?

The team's winning, the business is growing; is it time to relax? NO! When you feel you're getting the hang of it, keep going. Never think you're the best you can be. Continue to learn and continue to improve. If you're easily achieving your targets, consider that it might be they're set too low. I don't think you can ever reach the point of knowing how to be a good leader.

There are always opportunities to be better. I know that I learn something new every day. I have spoken to primary school groups, particularly about rowing the Atlantic, and they're always most entertained by the gory details. For example, is there a toilet on board? The answer that they love, of course, is no, there isn't. They look astonished, they giggle, they nudge each other, and I tell them about the bucket and having to be careful about not falling off, mid poo. This is usually met with screams of laughter and delight. But then, without fail, one child will ask a question or make a statement of such clarity and wisdom so far beyond their years, that I feel humbled and tearful. Always another lesson learned. 'Out of the mouths of babes' as the saying goes.

ROW YOUR OWN RACE

I think it's important to be authentic and confident. For me, it's not a sign of weakness to admit you're wrong or don't know something. Encourage your team to share their knowledge with you and with each other as everyone will benefit from collaboration. Something many of us don't say often enough are the words, 'Good job' and 'Well done'.

DEFINITION OF A GOOD LEADER

I'm sorry to say there isn't one. We all have our own definition of what makes a good leader. Because we're all so different and respond to different things, there isn't a one size fits all answer. Some will take to leadership easily, not sweating the small stuff and others struggle with it every day, worrying about how they are doing.

What I have learned about leadership is there's no right or wrong way to go about the different situations that arise. It's always complex, sometimes rewarding, often thankless, usually frustrating (especially if you tend to micromanage like I do), and there are even days when you just find it impossible and want only to bolt back under the bedclothes. But when your team starts to be consistently successful and come to you with innovative ideas, you realise that you're no longer flying by the seat of your pants. You can sit back and enjoy it, as long as it's only for a moment because there's always an issue around the next corner and you have to be ready to take it in your stride.

Good leaders ultimately enjoy everything about being a leader; the problems, the good times, the catastrophes, the problem solving and yes, even the difficult people issues. Confidence and enjoyment are contagious and if the leader radiates this, the team is far better for it.

To get to where I am and how I feel about my leadership took lots of trial and error, a lot of learning from my mistakes and the mistakes of others, along with some harsh lessons.

One event, in particular, makes me go cold even now when I think about it more than twenty years later.

CHAPTER 6
THE INDUSTRIAL TRIBUNAL AFFAIR

There was a father and son working in the business when I took over. The son was OK, but the Dad was militant, hard to work with, had a very negative attitude and challenged everything that was ever suggested. On top of this, certain items kept disappearing from the storeroom. I expected my other 15% shareholder to step up, investigate and sort things out. He didn't.

It felt like the Dad, I'm going to call him TJ for anonymity, had all sorts of little scams going. At the time, all the engineers had fuel cards and he would fill up on a Friday and again on the Monday. Obviously, the fuel cards were meant for work travel, not gadding about the country at the weekend. Then TJ started coming in late and spinning his wheels around in the carpark, things designed to push the boundaries and provoke a reaction. My huge expensive mistake, the one that still makes me cringe to this day, is that I didn't get rid of him when I assumed control in the January. I had the opportunity to make some personnel changes from the outset, but I didn't. I can only explain it by saying I was optimistic, eager to show I would do right by the existing staff and upon reflection was incredibly naive.

TJ's behaviour, the negative effect it was having on the rest of the team and the damage to the reputation of the business started taking a huge toll on me. I couldn't sleep at night and it was making me physically sick. I started drinking a lot most nights and during the wideawake night hours, poring over the books and financial projections for the business, I could see how under-financed we were. I had to do something but I'd over extended, borrowed and refinanced our mortgage (without telling my wife) to buy the business and now, because of this one troublemaker, it, or I, was probably going to go tits up.

The company was a member of the local and regional business groups and so I went to them for advice. They outlined the structure and process I'd need to follow in order to sack someone, but our contracts were terrible and because of the impact this was having on my health, and myself personally, I decided to act quickly. I fired TJ on a Friday. His son still worked for the business but was also quite threatening about what was likely to happen. I knew that TJ had a certain period of time in order to register a claim to an industrial tribunal and sure enough, two weeks before the deadline, I received the notification.

TJ was claiming unfair dismissal, public humiliation and loss of earnings to the tune of more than what was fair. I was instructed to attend and was advised to hire a solicitor, but simply could not afford the £3,000 per day that we were quoted.

I recognised when I took over the company that I needed someone with superior administration skills. One of the CVs I received was from a lady called Karen. She wasn't right for the role I'd advertised but I immediately recognised her skillset would make a wonderful Operations Manager. Karen was simply amazing and said she would build a book for our defence and could manage the whole process for the tribunal. In our ignorance and innocence, we thought we should easily be able to defend ourselves because we were in the right. How hard could it be?

In the run up to the tribunal date, TJ's son had bragged about how his Dad had been involved with two industrial tribunals against his previous employers and won on both occasions. By claiming on his house insurance, he had hired a lawyer on a no-win, no-fee basis. Obviously, this didn't bode well for us, and I started to realise we were in a seriously bad position. It didn't matter that we were right and that TJ deserved to be fired, we were almost certainly going to lose the case.

Our first appearance at the tribunal, before a panel of three, was a factual presentation of the case. Without any legal representation, we looked, and we were, massively unprepared. We were not capable of answering the questions and TJ's lawyer was able to make us look unprofessional very quickly. However, despite this, the panel did not feel able to come to a resolution, and we were adjourned with a date set for the defence some weeks later.

Back in the business, the atmosphere was toxic. TJ's son was stirring up the negativity and my health continued to nosedive. When we returned to the tribunal, I was told to present our defence with Karen there for moral support. Once inside we were told that as the defendant I couldn't do it all and had to have someone, normally a solicitor, to present our case. This is when Karen stepped in and took control of challenging TJ's statements. At her challenges, he stumbled over what he said, told outright lies, changed his story, was completely inconsistent and it was clear to me, at least, that much of his claim was fabricated. Surely, they would see he was a proven liar.

We got to lunchtime and the panel adjourned. When they returned, they had made some headway on their resolutions. They found the company at fault for having no discernible HR structure. I accepted these findings without question and accepted payment of the fines as I already knew from my conversations with the local business advisory service that I had failed in these areas.

The panel, though, had concerns over the many contradictions in the case and I was instructed to enter into mediation with TJ's solicitor. The lawyer said they would not back down on TJ's financial claim at all. Understanding that we were now into a straight negotiation, I offered to pay an amount I could live with, obviously much smaller than what was asked for. The lawyer representing TJ almost laughed in my face, but I could also see they weren't exactly convinced about the honesty of their client and, being paid a percentage of the win, it was in their best interest for me to pay as close to the maximum as possible.

As in all negotiations, it is critically important to understand the situation, and this is where my sales training and experience really kicked in. Despite her representing the opposition, I had remained friendly and spoken to his lawyer during the short breaks and adjournments. In speaking, I knew the lawyer needed to be at another much more lucrative case the following day, so I decided to run down the clock. As the time approached 4pm, I increased my offer slightly, and as time was running out she only hesitated for a second before accepting.

Leadership Wisdom

Leadership comes at a cost.

It was over. And although in every sense I lost, I considered it a valuable lesson that taught me so much more than the financial cost. It could have wiped me out both financially and in a business sense. Leadership comes at a cost, and I don't just mean financial, it often means taking steps that are hard and decisions that can affect friendships.

Leadership Wisdom

One of the costs of Leadership is loneliness.

This whole sorry exercise taught me some very grown-up lessons very quickly. I had hoped that running the company wouldn't be much different from working in the company. Yes, I realised I would be managing a whole raft of different things but essentially, I thought it would be business as usual. It wasn't. I was no longer just another member of the team, I was the leader. I had to stand alone because I was the one with the power to change the fate of the company, change the working practices, hire and fire. I became more decisive. I realised how my unwillingness to make changes when I took over had been perceived by some as weakness. Consequently, I put proper procedures in place for HR, and by now I knew the laws of dismissal inside out and vowed never to be taken advantage of in that way again.

I remembered how, on the day of TJ's initial dismissal, two people had come into the kitchen when I was making a cup of tea while I was still shaking. I looked at neither. One said, "nice one Matt!" and the other simply said, "what took you so long?"

Those two comments taught me a leadership lesson I have never forgotten. Now that TJ was gone, the atmosphere changed immediately. TJ was no longer there stirring up the negativity and spreading his toxic behaviour. His son quickly realised that trying to agitate on behalf of his Dad was a losing game and as he became less and less effective, the team started to function well in spite of him. Happily, within two months, he'd left the business of his own accord, making us short-staffed but the energy in the company increased and within three months we'd regrouped, become better organised and had started building a really positive culture with good momentum.

At the end of that difficult year, I bought a ticket to attend the annual conference of the business advice network. There was a great speaker from Apple talking all things HR, culture and people management. The only slide in his presentation summed up my experiences perfectly. It said:

I would rather have a hole in the business than an arsehole in the business.

I've never, ever forgotten it.

CHAPTER 7
LEADERSHIP DECISIONS – PUT YOUR STAMP ON EVERYTHING

As part of my decision-making process and revamping the company to achieve the growth that I wanted, I decided to make some key changes. I changed who the company banked with and started the search for a new accountant.

Various smartly dressed people started arriving for meetings. I hadn't realised that when I started interviewing candidates, the staff in engineering, who were under pressure to perform after TJ had left, thought I was interviewing potential new hires to replace him.

Leadership Wisdom

Put your stamp on everything, make your decisions visible and be accountable for changes.

By then, I hadn't even thought about finding a new engineer as I was so focused on what I wanted at a management level. It all became clear to me during a meeting with the team when, completely by chance, I stumbled upon one of the most motivational lines I have ever come up with.

The team was desperate for resources and my brain was working overtime to understand what they were thinking. To get myself off the hook I said, "I let you down last time and I haven't found someone good enough to work with you yet."

Right then and there, I made the decision to include them in all future recruitment discussions. Transparency matters and builds trust. Building and growing a business is not just about issuing orders from above, it's about getting everyone's buy-in so that the team is all working towards the same goal.

LEADERSHIP VISION

I've mentioned this before, but I want to repeat it again because it's so important. How do you get everyone working towards the goal you want? The answer is to clearly define and communicate it. A vision known by all staff becomes the circulatory system for the lifeblood of the company. I had a clear idea of how I wanted the company to operate and set out to make it known to every member of staff. I linked it to our sales targets, made sure everyone was moving in the right direction, built a timeline for the milestones we had to reach as well as the criteria needed to reach our goal.

This was when I started to define and document the early iterations of a sales and business growth methodology. I could see first-hand what worked in my company and what didn't. I knew that to be a good leader I needed to be firm but fair. I have always liked working in a team and running a company is no different. As a leader, I know I don't have all the answers and to me, building a team is about inviting the smart people who work for and with you to offer their opinions as well as ask questions.

I know as the leader you're expected to have all the answers, but in truth, and certainly for me, this is a ridiculous assumption. I do have a lot of ideas and always like to innovate but I never have all the answers. When I have an idea and want to pursue it, I ask my team, business colleagues and anyone whose opinion I value – I call this my 'Virtual Board' – what they think and ask for their input. I have the final say, but it's always an open forum for ideas and solutions. A collaborative leadership is healthier and more productive than leading by fear and being perceived as aloof.

The fact is if you're the leader you're almost always going to have the final say. There's absolutely no need to enforce your leadership position by pretending you're far above everyone else. I don't think any leader is. I am always prepared to listen and be vulnerable, I don't see it as weakness, it's the exact opposite. Showing vulnerability and standing up to lead, to be accountable and responsible shows strength and purpose.

CHAPTER 8
LEADERSHIP IS TOUGH

I t's often tough being the effective leader you want to be but sometimes you just have to suck it up and get on with it.

I've always loved rugby, having played since school and would've loved to have been good enough to be a professional. However, I knew early on that it was not meant to be and was content playing for my local club. As captain, a role I took seriously, I was responsible for ringing around and making sure we had a fit team for our upcoming fixtures.

Leadership Wisdom

Say the difficult stuff and say it succinctly, without blaming or shaming.

We had one teammate who was also a very successful businessperson; he was a good player, a huge guy, but often travelled the world limiting his availability. On one occasion, he answered the phone after a few rings, and I asked if he was available to play on Saturday. There was a slight delay on the line and he sounded far away so I asked where he was. "I'm in Denver, USA, Matt," he replied, but confirmed that, yes, he would be back in time for the 2:30 kick-off on Saturday.

I should have ruled him out immediately. Even if he could be back in time, after a long flight, stressed from travel and business, he might not be in the right frame of mind for a game. But he was a good mate, and with his size and weight, he was a great addition to our team.

Pretty early on we could tell it was going to be 'one of those games' and there were quite a few scuffles from the start. At times it got a bit ugly and the atmosphere of the home crowd was not friendly. The big guy, my teammate, usually a mild-mannered and good player, lost his cool after a tackle left him on the ground and stepped on the calf of one of the opposing team members. I didn't like what I saw and to be honest, was very surprised to witness it.

Rugby's a contact sport. There's nearly always some rough stuff happening and back then there were often some 'cheap shots' flying around as well as the occasional punch. Often there's no real malice involved, and most altercations are cleared up in the bar afterwards over a couple of beers.

What I witnessed that day, however, a big guy of around 20 stones stepping deliberately on the leg of a prone player went way beyond what was acceptable. After the match, I pulled him to one side and said I saw what he did, that I didn't like it, he was a much better player than that and it was not acceptable.

He was very contrite, and admitted he was exhausted and under considerable stress. His behaviour was totally out of character and I think we both learned a big lesson. I never again allowed someone to play if I thought there was any doubt about their readiness and availability, and I'm pretty sure he learned how easily stress can exacerbate any volatile situation.

Leadership Wisdom

Don't push yourself or your team beyond their endurance. A healthy work-life balance produces consistent and sustainable success.

I, too, had my own issues with stress induced physical ailments. They started around the time I took over the business and, making mistakes like keeping TJ when I could have easily and safely let him go, I continued pushing myself harder. I don't know how my wife, Sam, coped at all. I was very self-focused, my excuse being (not that I ever thought about it) that I was doing it for us, building a secure future for the family we planned to start at some point.

Except, the way I was going, I might not have lived to see it. I convinced myself I had to be in the office at 7am, I was drinking every night, sleeping too little, having blackouts and running on adrenaline. Sam thought I was heading for a heart attack, a nervous breakdown or both. Over the course of two years, I suffered fifteen bad incidents and saw a cardiologist who kept me under observation for two months.

Adding to these, during a fierce rugby match I suffered a knee to the temple, which gave me a concussion resulting in my having to be carried off the pitch. I remember lying on my side, vomiting and then being carted off to hospital. I was given an ECG, which revealed I had a left branch bundle block causing an erratic heartbeat. Luckily, I had no underlying heart disease, but it was definitely a huge wake-up call. In the following weeks, I had a couple of really bad head spins, first when I was in Brighton that forced me to grab some railings to save me from falling into the street. I sank to my knees to avoid landing in the gutter and cried a little. There, I had to wait it out, hanging on for dear life before I felt recovered enough to drive home. The last one happened the day Joseph, my son, was born. As he came into the world, I think I subconsciously realised that from now on, my family must be my first priority and my work, my ambition and my desire to prove myself came in a poor second. Here was a precious life that was a wake-up call for me.

A wise leader needs to lead by example. If I recognise that a good work-life balance is better for my team, then it must be better for me too, and I must show them that I know it.

Leadership Wisdom

Lead by example, but remember it's not a competition to be the best.

In my early years as a leader, I believed that in order to do so you had to be the best. I learned through experience that the best performer is not necessarily the best leader as the skills are very different. I've seen it in sports teams, in business and in every company I've helped over the years.

USING LEADERSHIP TO OVERCOME FEAR OF FAILURE

I have always taken risks, followed my gut feeling and known I didn't really fit into any set up I have seen or could imagine. When I was hopping from one thing to the next, I was trying to find a place that felt right for me. Sales was the first work that really felt like the right niche for me, just not the traditional sales environment as I never wanted to be another cog in a wheel. I have always felt stifled by strict regimes, too many rules and no flexibility to be innovative. I am still motivated by the fear of failure, and this is maximised when I feel boxed into a set routine and unable to break out of what's expected. I know now that this need to succeed is also motivated by an inferiority complex. Am I good enough? Can I really do this? Who gave me permission?

I knew the simple answer was that I am good enough, I can do it and I don't need anyone's permission. But knowing that intellectually and knowing it emotionally are wildly different. Often, I am pole-axed by self-doubt, and it drives me to prove to myself that I can do challenging things. I have learned that for me, trying everything and going all-in, I give myself the best chance of success. I never do anything half-heartedly. If I do something, I'm all-in. This has allowed me to choose the path I want to follow and given me a lot of different opportunities. It's possible to succeed in things you don't really want to do or have no passion for. But going all-in, you get to choose, not because you can't do something but because you can, if you want to.

As I have moved through my working life, I've been most successful when I've been able to forge my own path and lead my own team. As soon as I realised that I didn't have to be the best, I was free to hire people who *were* the best. If we were ever short staffed, and the team were agitating for more people, I would not be pushed into hiring someone who wasn't right and always returned to that one motivational quote I truly believe in: 'I haven't found someone good enough to work with you.'

After I'd been successful in increasing the company's sales and profits, I realised I'd reached the highest level I could with the set up at the time. I split the two divisions, the software and the IT, into two separate entities. I decided to sell the IT side (with the engineers) back to Mel, keeping the software business, which I duly merged with another software company.

I applied what I'd learnt, formalising and testing my sales methodology, and again after increasing the sales and profits, it was sold to a company backed by private equity investment.

We had achieved this despite going through the global financial crisis of 2008, that was leading to huge difficulties and the UK was facing the deepest recession since WW2. Despite all of this, it was an exciting and rewarding time for me. Across all industries, businesses at this time were either failing or stagnating, and I had not only managed to avoid any downturn in sales but also improved our financial situation against the worldwide trend. By all measures possible, I'd been hugely successful, buying into two companies, turning them around, making them huge successes and selling them as healthy going concerns.

I had proved myself and made a lot of money. I had made it and I was in a great place in my life. I was young, I had a beautiful, growing family, a nice house, lots of money in the bank, so why didn't I feel better?

About a month following the exit I suddenly realised I had no purpose. Once again, I felt I didn't quite fit in anywhere. I had great skills and knowledge, plenty of experience and I knew what I was good at. I was itching to be involved in something again and make a difference, but I had no direction, and I couldn't seem to find a place for myself.

Leadership Wisdom

When I've asked for feedback on my leadership, the most consistent answer is: He makes it happen!

It was 2012 and salvation came when a former client called and asked me to join his sales meeting and 'beat up my sales team' as he put it. It was something I knew I could do and maybe it would help get rid of this drifting feeling, though I didn't know anything about his company or their products so I was doubtful about how useful I could be. I told him so, but he was insistent and my whole future changed with what he said next: "No, Matt, I know you don't, and product doesn't matter. You bloody know how to run a sales team; you can get it done."

And in that moment the lights turned on and I knew with absolute clarity that this was exactly what I did know how to do. While he waited for my response, I grinned, 'yes', I said, "yes, I can." And I did, with the company going on to double its revenue over the next 3 years.

THE END OF MY PLAYING DAYS

Rugby has always been a passion for me, right from my earliest days listening to the more experienced players discussing strategy, tactics and different plays. As a young and inexperienced player, I wouldn't dare join in and mostly sat soaking it all up. Though gradually, as I started fitting into the team, earning my place, it felt like the combined wisdom and experience of the more senior guys was being poured into me, and it was thrilling to be part of it all. I loved playing the game, watching it and reading about it. I was especially interested in everything about those special players who got the chance to be captain and lead the team.

Aged 40, after playing for almost as long as I could remember, I was now carrying niggling injuries and it was taking longer and longer to recover after a match. How was it possible that time had gone so quickly? I still had the thirst to play, but there was nothing I could do to keep up with the physical demands of playing a full game. I had no option but to hang up my playing boots and switch my energies towards coaching the junior teams at my local club.

As Sam and I now had two young children, it was a great way to stay involved and share what I'd learned in my more than 20 years of playing and captaining teams. It was also a good way of introducing Joseph and Mollie to the great game that had always been so kind to me. Being around the club while involved with coaching was great, but it wasn't enough for me. I needed more.

Leadership Wisdom

It's impossible to lead if you don't have a team. A good leader will actively look for opportunities to make a difference.

My mate, Rob, who gave up playing at the same time as me, recommended I participate in a triathlon. On hearing the suggestion, I replied, "I'm a very weak swimmer, literally only able to do head up breaststroke, I'm a lumpy runner and don't really enjoy it, and I haven't been on a bike since my paper round." He grinned and said, "Yep, I know, but you're one stubborn bastard!"

Competing appealed to me so I trained hard, entered and completed a few triathlons, progressing from sprint distance to Olympic distance but, aged over 40, I realised I wasn't going to get any faster so decided instead to go longer. After completing five half-Ironman events, the mystique and allure of the mythical 'Ironman' wouldn't go away. Two years after completing my first sprint triathlon, I crossed the finish line having completed the Ironman in Germany. My name was announced as I crossed the line and it was a huge moment.

Again, I had made friends with other competitors, attended training, entered events and finished with respectable placings. However, there was something missing; the team spirit, that feeling of leading a team, of playing an important part in the success of a group of people with different skills and talents that together make up more than the sum of their parts. Without this I felt empty and wanted to know what I could do that would be challenging, involve leading a team and not completely destroy me physically.

I live on the coast and the more I swam, the more I enjoyed open water swimming; the freedom, the wildness and looking out at the sea. One day, I thought *I wonder if I could swim to France?* At that, I knew what I wanted to do; *I'm going to swim the English Channel!*

An adventure of a lifetime, I was quite sure that if I managed it, I'd never want to do it again! But such an experience, I knew for myself, wouldn't work as a solo but leading a team would hit the right spot. I mentioned it to Sam and at first, she was horrified, pointing out I hadn't been swimming all that long before dismissing it as something that would probably never happen, mostly because I'd never find three other people mad enough to be involved.

It wasn't long before I'd enlisted three people who agreed to give it a go. And we were on! Our team was:

Coxy, who I'd met a few years earlier at a triathlon training camp, and we'd hit it off; great guy, good swimmer.

Sandra, put forward by her regular swimming friend, Coxy.

BC, a good friend, and person I'd met through business dealing. I knew BC enjoyed swimming and would be up for a challenge.

Swimming the English Channel is highly regulated with many rules. These cover what you wear, trunks for men and one-piece swimsuit for women. Proof you've survived a qualification swim in temperatures below 15C, and many others. There are so many rules and regulations to comply with before you're allowed to register for the opportunity to take part that it forces you to understand just how dangerous it can be.

Before our attempt, we all trained for a year. I just hoped we were ready.

CHAPTER 9
THE CHANNEL SWIM

I didn't really know what to expect and was a sleepless bundle of nerves in the 24 hours before our attempt. When it was all over and we were safe, dry, salty-lipped and so overtired we could barely sleep, I retired to my room and wrote three pages of notes about how I'd felt. I never intended to show anyone, which might explain the swearing, but it was important to me to record how hard it was, the extreme nature of the challenge and in some way, provide proof for myself that I had actually done it. So, here are my notes, written in a more readable format and with all the swearing intact.

I'm still incredibly proud to have achieved this. I'm very glad I made these notes because I still find it hard to think about without becoming emotional and this helps me remember.

Dover. The day of our Channel swim. The clouds were heavy and there was a residual swell still rolling in. I pulled up my hood against the wind, shivering. We'd met at BC's hired cottage the night before and I'd set my alarm for 1:45am, needing to be at the boat in Dover by 2:30am. After only four hours sleep, I'd woken not knowing where I was. I'd lain in bed, trying to work out what the fuck I was doing there, doubting everything. There was burnt porridge for breakfast and eating it was hard work so I added honey and blueberries, but I was still struggling because of my nerves.

We arrived at the harbour only to discover there'd been a last-minute switch of boats from the Gallivant to the Sea Satin. Our skipper, Lance, is the son of the skipper on the Gallivant. I didn't know whether to think this was good or bad luck for our attempt.

Lance and his crew seemed like a great group, were genuinely glad to be part of our crossing attempt and wanted us to succeed. I felt lightheaded, nauseous and couldn't focus. My head was filled with a secret hope that our attempt would be cancelled due to poor weather conditions. No such luck. It was up to us, our decision. We were told we had a 24-hour weather window to go for it or else we'd have to delay until September. As a team, we agreed to go for it. We had our briefing and filled out the relevant questionnaire details. We declared our swim order, which had to be strictly adhered to, and any variation would see us disqualified.

We climbed into the support boat, the Sea Satin, and slipped our moorings. We went around the harbour wall and headed out to sea before steaming gently towards Samphire Hoe, our set off point. A big swell was still rolling in from the day before and I could feel my whole body crawling with anxiety. A part of me was still secretly hoping that our attempt would be called off due to the swell. I pulled my hood closer to hide my face in case the others could read what I was thinking and tried to focus.

Leadership Wisdom

Leaders need to appear confident. Even if you're not feeling it, fall back on your training, knowledge and experience, and let your team give you the confidence you need.

In the half light of early dawn, we arrived at Samphire Hoe to start the swim in the half light of near dawn. As the leader, I had elected to be the first swimmer. I was told to clip on my lights, don my goggles, strip down to my trunks and prepare to get into the water. All I could think was *WTF am I doing?*

I was in such a state that later, I was unable to recall the feel and temperature of the water. From the boat to the beach, I swam like a madman, face planting on the pebbles, and tried to stand and pretend I was in control, though I couldn't stop my legs from shaking. My guts were roiling with nerves and adrenaline as I stepped clear of the water line and onto the pebbles that hurt my feet.

Fortunately, I had no time to dwell on how I was feeling because the hooter sounded, and it was on!

No turning back, no delay, I plunged straight back into the shallow surf breaking on the shore, taking in a couple of slugs of seawater in the first couple of strokes. I tried to count to sixty to mark a minute, but I couldn't concentrate. I had to use all my focus so that I didn't swallow gulps of salt water every time I needed to breathe. I was struggling with retching, bringing up the sea water in my stomach that I'd inhaled to conceal the vomiting from the others by ducking beneath the water. Although I'd been determined to lead by example, I realised I was already out of my depth, both literally and metaphorically. Anxiety had taken hold of me and I told myself that I'm not tough enough for this, that I'm sinking. The only way to take back control was to shout at myself so between breaths and mouthfuls of seawater, I shouted, "just swim, don't you fucking dare let the team down." Occasionally, I added, "you'll be able to breathe properly later, just swim, just swim, just swim." I tried desperately to believe that it would help because I wasn't even halfway through my first leg and I was already ill from the seawater I'd swallowed. Every stroke meant I needed to retch, and my whole body was screaming out to stop, but I refused to give in, and I counted every second to the sound of my own inner mantra: keep going, keep going, keep going…

The swell was terrible and frequently pushed me upright. The bigger swells made it very clear to me that my swimming ability might catch me out unless I was able to maintain focus.

I saw my first jellyfish and decided not to mention it because the fear of them can be a terrible distraction for a swimmer, and if the others were finding their first leg as difficult and challenging as I was then I didn't want to add to their burden.

Leadership Wisdom

Break difficult tasks into smaller tasks, complete them with focus and determination.

I avoided the wind as much as possible by remaining close to the port side of the boat. Sometimes I came to within 5-10 metres, but had to make sure I didn't touch it because that would mean disqualification, and then the team attempt would be over. After the longest thirty minutes of my life, I saw the red towel waving to signal I was halfway through my first set. Although I was relieved to see it, I had hoped that somehow I'd missed it and the next thing I'd see would be BC getting ready to enter next. Disappointment and not a little despair filled me as I thought, *is that all?* I had hoped so much that my first swim would nearly be over. It was so disheartening. I felt like time was slowing down and my muscles were already screaming. I desperately needed to get out of the water, have time to calm myself and regain my physical and mental strength. Again, I started counting to sixty seconds and told myself that either way, I had survived through the worst of my first stint. I decided to use these blocks to try to understand what twenty minutes swimming actually felt like. How many breaths, how many strokes. I tried to focus on it, but I was already looking to see if BC was starting to prepare and lost count.

During the harbour briefing, the skipper had said that he would give us ten minutes notice for the next swimmer to get ready. I was so focused on willing BC to stand that I was completely disoriented. Surely, it was time, surely he should be getting ready by now. What seemed like hours later, but was in fact mere minutes, I finally saw him starting his preparation for his first swim.

At last, only ten minutes to go. And then I saw the red towel for the five-minute warning. What a huge relief! I can't remember who was waving it, only what joy I felt to see it. Only five more minutes and I would be safely on the boat, out of this hell. I started counting down my final 300 seconds and wondered if I'd get to 300, or was I counting too slowly? Better too slow, I decided, than too fast and reach the target and still be swimming. Then I lost count, and my concentration was thumped out of me by a wave that hit me and sent a slug of water straight down my throat just as I was taking a breath. All over again, I felt like I was going to vomit, but I didn't want anyone to see me duck under the water, so I forced myself to suppress it.

Leadership Wisdom

Leading by example means giving the team confidence. Don't overshare difficulties that might be unique to you, they won't be helpful.

Finally, the hooter sounded, and I saw BC jump in. I couldn't believe how calm and eager he looked when I felt like I'd been punched and pummelled by a heavyweight opponent. Was it possible he was looking forward to this whole thing? I swam towards the boat's stern and climbed the ladder, my legs as weak as the smile I'd plastered across my face to greet the others.

Sandra and Coxy wrapped me in towels before congratulating me on setting a good pace and getting us off to a great start. I had barely heard what they were saying, and I was glad they didn't realise how thankful I was to be back on the boat. I was shaking so hard that I couldn't believe they didn't notice; it was partly from the cold, part adrenaline and part relief in my muscles to have some respite from the strength of the waves and the tide. All I could think was that my first stint was over, I hadn't let the team down and they seemed unaware of the difficulty and doubts that I'd experienced. Thank fuck for that!

The minutes ticked by so fast, but I started to calm down. I watched BC in the water, and he looked like he was powering along, doing really well. I smiled realising it was likely he was thinking and feeling exactly as I had. I knew the others would have been watching me thinking I was doing really well, even if I didn't feel it. While I got dressed, Sandra made me a cup of tea with ginger biscuits. I knew from my fishing trawler days that ginger biscuits were supposed to help with motion sickness and as I was still feeling the effects of swallowing so much saltwater,

I hoped there was a chance they might help with the awful nausea now.

Leadership Wisdom

Remember the words: Good Job and Well Done!

Especially at the beginning of a hard journey.

BC looked really strong in the water and was putting in a good shift, so I went to chat with the crew. They asked me about my swim, but I didn't want to divulge how difficult I found it, so I lied, shrugging it off and telling them it wasn't too bad. As the words spilled from my lips, an overwhelming realisation hit me like a tidal wave; we were in for a miserably long and incredibly cold, hard day and it had only just begun.

Feeling daunted by the huge task ahead, I returned to where Coxy and Sandra were sitting. It barely registered when they again congratulated me on a giving us a good start and I was thankful they didn't know how shit I felt. I noticed Coxy looked very pale and he admitted he was not feeling the best, perhaps a touch of seasickness.

Leadership Wisdom

Learn quickly from the impressive behaviour of others.

I was very aware that if one person quit then we would all be out because the team would be disqualified. I didn't want to reveal the struggle that I'd experienced because it wouldn't help him at all so instead I told him to keep an eye on the horizon and I worked on ways to encourage him, which I'm not sure he needed. In many ways it really helped me because I had to step out of my own head and be the leader. I deliberated over how to help him, and what to say, and so I dug deep to put myself mentally back in the water to better visualise what had helped me through it. It reinforced what I suspected. What we see in others and what we assume they're feeling is usually very far from what they think we're seeing and what they're actually feeling. It was up to me as the leader and first swimmer to protect Sandra and Coxy from my experience, to help them with *their* first swim. I knew for certain that hearing my private fears and the horror of my first leg wouldn't help them. Carrying thoughts of my anxiety and my struggle into the water could only add to their own. I knew it would be the same for BC. Whatever he was going through, he wouldn't lay it on us. I started to work on projecting an air of (what I hoped was) understated confidence to Sandra and Coxy. I think it helped me more than them.

BC continued putting in a very strong and smooth stint. He looked powerful in the water, strong and confident, really up for anything it might throw at him. When the hooter went, Sandra's turn to dive off the back of the boat, but when she did her swimsuit got caught and was pulled down to her waist. She was amazing, totally unfazed by it and carried on swimming topless in the water. I was full of admiration and still am as she showed incredible determination and a will to succeed. Her strength was a huge lesson for me. As I watched Sandra, and having seen BC, crack on, I realised I was with strong people. With a jolt, I knew that in my first stint I had also shown strength and determination to overcome my feelings. It was a comfort knowing that today I just needed to do my job and that would be more than enough, and their strength gave me strength and renewed motivation. It helped Coxy too as he started feeling better and was already preparing for his first swim.

Leadership Wisdom

Guide the team with emotional intelligence, understand when to speak and when to keep silent.

I saw Sandra take a couple of big slugs of seawater, but she carried on regardless as though fighting against fierce currents in the English Channel was the most normal thing in the world. I saw how tough she was, powering through the waves, and it helped me rise above my anxiety of feeling like I didn't belong. For the first time since boarding the boat, I knew I could do this.

Despite feeling nauseous I ate the first of my cheese and marmite sandwiches as Coxy began covering himself with sun cream. I couldn't help grinning at the sight. The weather was bloody awful, but there was a method to his seeming madness, sunscreen is also supposed to have an anti-jellyfish quality.

I wasn't convinced it would help because if the sting was going to happen, surely the jellyfish would only find out later that it doesn't like the cream. Nevertheless, Coxy kept mumbling that he hates jellyfish and I reckoned that if it helped bring him peace of mind then it was worth the effort. I stifled my laugh though because, slathered in white cream, he looked like a typical British tourist on his first trip to Benidorm, and I understood that this was his way of mentally preparing for his daunting first swim. Going last was always going to be the most difficult slot. It had its own unique difficulties. The long wait, the build-up of apprehension, watching us all swallowing water, shivering from cold, pale as ghosts as we dried ourselves and warmed up. None of us wanted to let the team down, swimming last in the relay meant Coxy was the only one yet to prove himself.

The hooter went and Coxy jumped in. Right from his very first stroke, it was clear to me that both he and Sandra, as well as BC, are so much better swimmers, and BC is stronger and steadier than me. Watching them gave me a shiver of anxiety and the feeling that I was by far the weakest swimmer.

It is an unsettling thought, and I knew I had to relax during my next swim and let the anxiety go. I may not be as proficient as them, but I have the will to pull my weight and refuse to let down the team.

The three hours flew by, and it didn't seem possible that it was time for me to get ready to go in again. My trunks, still where I'd left them in a corner of the deck, felt cold and horrible. A shiver ran through me just looking at them. Fuck it! I should have hung them up.

It seemed merely a blink before it was my turn again to jump in. I started counting to 60 straight away, but this time I was so much calmer, managing to breathe without swallowing water. I easily got into the groove and this time the sea didn't feel quite so bad. Having worried about not being able to relax, it happened naturally, and I was soon able to think of other stuff because I didn't have to focus on my survival. The only downside was that all I *could* think about was the cold!

Before I knew it, I saw, with astonishment, the 30-minute towel and for the first time I felt like I deserved to be in the team. I felt strong and my swimming was confident. I counted my way through another twenty minutes and was very happy to see BC getting ready for his second stretch. I relaxed a bit too much, though, and my over-confidence made me less vigilant as I had to abruptly change course to weave between two jellyfish. It was a scarily close call as I was within only a couple of seconds of ploughing straight into them, and it was only with the greatest of fortune I was able to avoid them both.

Thankful to see the 5-minute towel waving, the jellyfish adrenaline burst started to abate and with it came extreme tiredness. I started my count to 300, only getting to 120 when the hooter blasted out. BC was back in the water, and I swam to the ladder at the back of the boat feeling colder than before as I struggled to haul myself up the ladder.

Eventually, I clambered on board, weak but not as much as I was after my first stint. Despite feeling cold, I wasn't shaking this time or feeling nauseous, and I grinned to myself knowing without any hesitation that I was definitely good enough to be part of this team.

It would be another three hours before I was called back to the water so in the meantime I dressed in five layers to keep warm. Meanwhile, I was handed a Cup-a-Soup with pasta, which tasted disgusting, though I knew it would help make me feel warm and energised so I persevered and forced it down.

Two other boats with hopeful relay teams of Channel swimmers had left at around the same time as us, but they were a long way behind. I couldn't help but feel that, however painful I was finding the conditions, at least we were doing better than them. Watching from the safety of the boat, I could see that every member of our team was doing a cracking job with their second stints and from my perspective, the hours were uneventful. Each time the hooter blasted following the completion of an hour in the turbulent sea, everyone on the boat would rally around and help the exhausted swimmer, providing warmth and refreshments.

At this point, we had entered the shipping lanes and our boat suddenly seemed very small. Swimming in the cold, unforgiving English Channel, passing some enormous container ships, was quite an experience.

However, the crew weren't phased and stayed down below cooking up bacon, sausages, and beans. The smell started wafting temptingly around the boat and reminded me that for them, this journey was nothing exceptional but just another working day, and that was hard to equate with what our swim team was going through emotionally.

I went back on deck to speak to Lance, the skipper. I wanted to find out where we were, his estimate of how much further we had to go and his impression of how we were doing.

I hoped and perhaps expected him to be invested in our success, even if only a little. He didn't give much away except that we'd reached about mid-Channel. He sounded very practical in his assessment and said we still had a lot of work ahead to complete a successful attempt. At first, it seemed like he was uninterested in our success or potential failure, but I began to understand that he could see how elated we were to complete our second stints after the shock of our first ones. It may have been my first time, but it wasn't his, and he knew how over-confidence might set us back and undermine our focus. At the time it seemed like a pessimistic view, though on reflection it gave me a helpful and necessary perspective.

In the distance, looking back towards England, I could still see Dover quite clearly and approaching hour nine of our swim there was still no sign of France. How could that be possible?

It dawned on me that my three hours of rest was nearly over and I should have been preparing for my return to the water.

We were now past mid-Channel, and the wind was howling at a stiff 16-18 knots. Lance told me the conditions were now so bad that we wouldn't have been allowed to start the attempt had it been like this back in Dover, though as we'd now come so far, we were allowed to continue.

By now we were all feeling quite low and less optimistic. I thought privately, though, that we'd succeed, literally, come hell or high water.

The wind was now against the tide and the sea was very rough. I watched as Coxy successfully finished his second stint like the champion that he is, though soon enough it was my turn once more.

This time, it immediately felt different because now I was swimming in a storm and was fighting against the sea, which was hard as swimming a single length sprint, flat out as fast as I could at the pool. If I saw conditions like this at the beach, I wouldn't even start training, I'd pack up and go home. How the hell were we even swimming in this tempestuous sea?

Leadership Wisdom

Recognise low points and practice ways to overcome them. Focus on completing the tasks one by one. The act of finishing one task after another builds confidence and will lead you out of a crisis.

I started moaning to myself, overcome with self-pity. The doubting voice in my head took over, taunting me, *you're not cut out for this, no one would blame you for quitting now, do it, it's so much tougher now, it's un-swimmable, it's too hard, conditions are so much worse now.*

Aborting the attempt would have been understandable.

But the voice was brutally suppressed when I gulped a mouthful of seawater that went straight to the pit of my stomach.

Knowing the retching was about to commence, I suddenly resented my weakness and found a new determination to stop that critical undermining voice, pausing and shouting into the wind, "toughen up you wanker!"

The retching started and the water came straight back up, leaving a horrible salty residue in my mouth. I felt myself descending into a real meltdown and shouted, "what the fuck am I doing? I want to get out, I want to get out now!" But the wind took my words, and they sank into the vastness of the sea.

Somehow, because the only option was, actually, to climb out and sink the team, I found a shred of strength to concentrate. I spoke harshly to myself, quitting is not an option, not yet. I tricked myself by leaving it as an option for later. I told myself, *you're the leader of this team. You must lead the way, or you're not a leader at all. Yes, it's tough, yes, it's so much tougher than it should be, but it is what it is.* And I knew I had to deal with the task at hand, completing my hour, one stroke after another. I had to dig deep and concentrate on just getting two, then three, then four good breaths, in and out, and begin calming myself down. I told myself to stop fucking moaning, it was the same for everyone in the team, I must be strong, I can do it, and I will lead by example.

The sea felt leaden, it looked terrifying. It was at its heaviest, and I shouted at myself under the water, "you didn't sign up for this because it was going to be easy, you signed up because it would be hard! You're doing this because you can." I repeated it over and over, silently, mentally and shouting it into the wind. It worked and for the first time in the stint, I really started to believe it.

When I saw the 30-minute towel and put my thumb up to Sandra, I knew how important it was for me to look confident leading the way. I thought I saw her grin and knew what it meant to the team. Maybe I *was* made for leadership after all?

The next twenty minutes sped by. I kept arguing with myself and became more and more angry when the whiny voice told me I couldn't do it. Yes, I can, yes, I can, yes, I can, became my mantra. And then, yes, I can, just fucking watch me! Soon enough I could see BC getting his swim cap on and knew I must be close to getting out, though by now I was nowhere near as desperate as before. Finally, Sandra waved the five-minute towel and I began counting down my 300 seconds.

Then the horn split the air, BC was in the water and for the first time I started feeling relaxed because I knew the team was going to make it.

I was ecstatic to leave the water and dried myself quickly, grabbing hold of BC's dry robe unsure whether he'd decided he didn't need it or, discreetly and generously, he'd left it for me.

I wondered at his perception and thought that, perhaps, he too saw the conditions, my fight with the water and knew how much I needed it. What a team player. What a team.

Leadership Wisdom

Don't forget to reward yourself, it's not just the team that needs a pat on the back.

The weather was horrible sitting on the boat, almost as wet as being in the water. I knew I'd done a good hour and deserved a rest. As always, I watched as BC powered on, strong and seemingly effortless in the worst of the weather. He put in a good shift and I was full of admiration for how controlled he looked, how confident and steady.

Then, finally, when I glanced up I was convinced the silhouette of the French coast lingered on the horizon. Perhaps it was hope deceiving me, but I crossed my fingers all the same.

I ate the last of my last sandwiches and, one by one, Sandra and Coxy took their next stints. Sandra, as always, looked as though she was swimming at the pool; elegant, cool and smooth. Coxy, Sandra and BC all looked like they coped well with the conditions and swam without any of the drama that I went through. I watched each of them in the water, looking for clues, and noticed they also swallowed their fair share of water, just as I did.

I couldn't begin to know what they were going through mentally, and just like I didn't share what I went through with them, if they were feeling unsure, I didn't know it.

Approaching a big water buoy, Lance announced we had reached a 3-mile marker to land. We passed it on our port side but within minutes, it was behind us on starboard, such was our movement, while we continued being battered by the wind and tide, at the mercy of the elements like a toy boat in an angry toddler's bath.

I scanned the horizon to see if I could spot the Cap Gris-Nez lighthouse on the cliffs above the beach where we were due to come ashore. I had read that on a clear day, you could see the English coast from the headland though unfortunately, that wouldn't be possible in these terrible conditions.

Lance told Coxy to put in a big set as we were closing on our finish line. He prepared like a man on a mission, saying he reckoned that if this was indeed going to be his last shift, he was going to make it count.

I started to wonder if I would need to swim again and began desperately to hope not. I found it increasingly hard to face the mental hurdle of getting in, but conversely, found it easier each time I was in to talk myself through the anxiety. Jason and Lance were running a book with Sandra, the odds-on favourite to swim ashore. That definitely meant two more hours of swimming, with me next up. Bollocks!

Coxy, as always, put in a big shift, taking us to within two miles of France. I prepared to go back in, though this time the water was not quite so rough, and I could tell by the colour and change in temperature we were in shallower depths.

My spirits lifted and my confidence grew because I could feel the tide was with me, even though we were going across the bay from right to left. I, too, wanted to put in a Herculean effort as this would be my last shift so I made the conscious decision to swim as hard and as fast as I could for the entirety of the hour. I told myself I was not going to search the horizon; I was going to be head down and focused, body and soul, on swimming hard. If I could do it, it would be, it had to be, and absolutely, definitely would be my last set.

Leadership Wisdom

If you're finding the going tough, adjust your mindset. Focus on a different aspect that will bring your goal closer.

Armed with this new mindset, my new goal and feeling better in the warmer water, I even started enjoying myself, knowing that I was getting us closer.

I knew it wouldn't be me going ashore at the finish line; I didn't even figure in Lance and the crews' betting, and I surprised myself by realising that I really didn't care at all.

Soon enough, the 30-minute towel came and went, and then it seemed like no time at all before I could see BC getting ready. I knew I'd given my best and that my work was nearly done - thank fuck!

Sandra and Coxy were sitting at the bow and waved the five-minute towel. I upped my game, muscles screaming as I swam as hard as I could, shouting to myself "Yes! Yes! Yes! – Channel Swimmer!"

The hooter blasted loud and long, and I grasped the ladder. I felt strong and powerful, buoyed by the water until I climbed a few rungs up and then I realised how much the stint has exhausted me. I eventually pulled myself to the top, trying not to topple back into the water, with barely the energy to climb aboard.

I needed to sit down and get warm. I was so happy to strip off my cold, wet trunks, hoping never in my life to wear them again. When I was dressed and feeling better, Coxy and Sandra said they reckoned we all ought to swim to shore at the end to celebrate. My heart sank, my knackered muscles felt like blancmange. How could I tell them I'd had enough, both mentally and physically, and that I just didn't think I could wear my cold trunks again. All I could think was *who fucking cares who gets to be the one making it to the beach, we're a team, we've all done this together. BC could do the finish alone, just like I did the start alone.*

I started to mutter about the team and...but they stopped me in my grumpy tracks. They impressed on me that this would never happen again. This team, this swim, these conditions, we would never have this experience together again. Swimming to France in awful conditions, standing together, our team, on the beach, a joint effort, each of us giving our all to the team. They were so earnest and convincing that it only took me a moment to realise they were right. I was overwhelmed by the cold and the exhaustion, but as they made me look past that, I agreed with them and suddenly wanted it as much as they did. All for one, one for all!

We were drifting along the beach as we got closer and I started to wonder whether BC would be the one making it to shore, or would Jason and Lance be right and Sandra would be the one with the honour? All we could do was wait and watch, and I wondered what was going through BC's mind as he swam. Would he mind not being the one to finish after having got so close or would he, like me, just be relieved his stint was over?

A kite surfer appeared alongside the boat, dangerously close, to ask what we were doing. Coxy was about to tell him to fuck off in the typical English way, though luckily we all dug deep to our better selves and smiled and waved. We felt friendly and European, it made us feel good.

Lance joined us on the deck to explain the finishing rules in more detail, and the process for reaching the beach. It would be BC going ashore and we were allowed to join him in the water, though BC had to be the one touching the beach first. We had to remain behind him until the swim was officially adjudicated to be finished or our team would be disqualified.

Gary, a member of the Sea Satin crew, launched the inflatable and dropped back a little from the boat for the final push. Lance told Sandra to enter the water and BC slowed as he glanced up in surprise, exhaustion radiating from him. He had no idea what was going on so we shouted at him to continue swimming. He put in his final effort and Sandra followed, keeping well behind him.

I was still grumpy about putting on my cold, wet trunks having only just warmed up, and I kept Coxy waiting until we were only about 50 metres short of the beach. We both jumped in, and I was astonished by how warm and lovely the water felt. In an instant, all my reservations about getting back into the water disappeared and I enjoyed the feeling of being buoyed by the gentle swell as we leisurely swam towards the beach, ensuring to keep well clear of BC in our enthusiasm to get ashore.

Leadership Wisdom

Celebrate success with the team. Take the time to share the achievement and your role in it.

BC kept swimming until he suddenly realised he was in shallow water and able to stand. We watched him as he made his way up the beach, holding back as he left the water then Coxy and I shared a quick hug in the shallows as Sandra waded onto the sand. I said to Coxy, "I can't believe we did that!"

Then, exhaustion forgotten, we ran up the beach. I grabbed hold of BC and Sandra and lifted my goggles, choking with emotion. I couldn't get my head around it; we'd just swum the English Channel, we were walking on the beach in France, and I couldn't believe it. We did it, we bloody well did it!

There were a few locals on the beach, one of whom took photos and, incredibly, told us he knew Lance and that they were friends on Facebook. As they say, it's a small world. He said he would post the images, allowing Lance to tag us, and I desperately hoped he would because I wanted those pictures that would serve as proof we did it, that *I* did it.

People started gathering around us and we must have looked like lunatics hugging and shouting; classic mad dogs and Englishmen (and one Australian). They were interested in knowing what we'd just done, as well as how long it took, though at the time nobody knew the answer to that.

Another person looked straight at me and asked *why, what made you do it?* In that moment, finding the words to utter a coherent response was impossible so instead I just kept grinning and shouting, "we did it!"

Pretty soon it was time to return to the boat. I quickly grabbed a French pebble for my children, tucking it into my trunks for safety before running back into the surf towards the inflatable.

Unfortunately, as the waves hit me, the pebble fell out through the bottom of my trunks. Panicking, I struggled to find it, trying to see through the water, splashing it up as I tried to push it out of the way. I was just about to give up when I found it in the sand and grabbed it. I asked Gary in the inflatable to look after it for me so I could swim to the boat.

He nodded with a gentle smile and tucked it securely inside his warm, dry pocket, no doubt assuming the exhaustion had unhinged me.

Leadership Wisdom

Thank the people who've been on the journey with you. You made it happen, but you didn't do it by yourself.

I plunged back into the water and hoped it would be for the last time, for a long time, and swam towards the Sea Satin. When I was once again safely aboard, I was absolutely certain, as the others emerged at the top of the ladder, that we were all saying a silent prayer of thanks that we could get dry, dressed, warm and throw our wet swimwear into the bottom of a bag and not think about it again.

Once we were all sitting comfortably, we congratulated ourselves, congratulated each other and thanked the skipper and crew who had been absolutely magnificent. We knew we couldn't have done it without their practical help, but they had given us more than that, they had kept us on track, kept us steady and believed in us, even through the depths of our uncertainty.

I felt fully relaxed, a sense of achievement warming every part of me, and could sit back and enjoy the journey back to Dover.

We checked our live Facebook stream that had kept our friends and family updated since we began nearly 14 hours ago. The feed was going crazy now it had registered we'd successfully finished our crossing.

We quickly passed the other boats that were still struggling to get their swimmers ashore in France, and my heart went out to them. I silently hoped they would make it safely ashore soon.

Despite our exhaustion, we were all unable to stop grinning. Wanting only to return to dry land and impatient with our progress, I decided to try and sleep in one of the bunks below deck. I was soon warm and snug in a sleeping bag, but sheer excitement, more powerful than the exhaustion, wouldn't let me doze off. In the end I gave up trying to sleep and just enjoyed laying there, safe and warm, feeling the rhythmic swell as the boat fought its way home through the cold, inhospitable waves.

I happily relinquished any thoughts about the weather and what it might or might not do. It could blow a gale, lash with rain, storm, throw anything at us and it still couldn't touch us because we'd made it. We had swum the English Channel, and my team were fucking champions!

When we were about half an hour from Dover, I went back on deck. The sky was incredible with all sorts of unusual cloud formations, beautiful but odd. I felt superstitious and asked myself if they were a sign. I knew I was exhausted and likely being fanciful, so I put it down to the extreme emotions of the day, though it still seemed like some cosmic acknowledgement of what we'd achieved. If I'd said those thoughts out loud to the others, I suspected they'd have laughed or thought I'd gone off my rocker, so I kept them to myself.

Watching the swell of the water and the fast-moving clouds, it brought it home to me how hard it had been to fight the weather and the tides just to make it across the Channel. I also understood how lucky we'd been catching the weather window that had allowed us to make our attempt.

At long last, we pulled into the loading area at Dover and BC's wife and son were there to greet us. We unloaded the boat and passed on our eternal and effusive thanks to the magnificent crew and posed for photos with them and each other.

I was back on dry land and we had done it. We had swum the English Channel. I had been on the beach in Samphire Hoe, England, and then fourteen hours later, exhausted from swimming, I had stepped ashore in Cap Gris-Nez, France. What an achievement!

Leadership Wisdom

Learn from every experience. A post event review will teach you a lot about yourself, your leadership and how to be even better next time.

I thought about what a great team we were and realised that it wasn't by chance. We had made that team by training together. We had thoroughly committed to each other. We lived and breathed what we felt, which was very much all for one and one for all, no question. We had developed a great team spirit, each of us had given it our all for the sake of the others and not a single one of us had been willing to let the others down. I was so proud of everyone and so pleased to have been a part of it.

After a short car ride, we arrived back at the cottage BC had rented for us. The joy of having a warm shower was incredible. I washed the inside of my mouth and thoroughly brushed my teeth, wondering if I'd ever lose the ever-present taste and feel of salt. It was so good to put on clean, dry clothes and be properly warm once again and still, I just couldn't stop grinning, saying to myself over and over, "we fucking did it!"

BC's wife cooked us a great supper. At first, I struggled to eat, exhaustion and that salty taste in my mouth preventing me, but the lovely atmosphere, the camaraderie and the need for the warm food overtook me and I soon helped myself to more and more roast potatoes. We all started to relax into the evening and to celebrate, BC cracked open the most expensive bottle of Australian wine I've ever tasted. It was, of course, totally wasted on us, a team of exhausted salty mouthed individuals but, what the hell, we wanted to celebrate.

We knew how rare a day like this was, a once-in-a-lifetime event. Those people, that team, that feeling wouldn't come around again. Soon we would go back to being individuals again, but for that precious time, we had shared something life-changing, and it deserved to be celebrated.

Pretty quickly, the warmth, the good food and the wine overcame us and we all started to flag. The adrenalin was at last releasing its hold on us all, and I felt so tired I wondered if I could even make it to bed and had to force myself to take the short steps to my room. The others were the same, almost falling asleep as we walked. Once I was lying in my bed though, in the calm quiet, my extreme tiredness started to disappear. I grinned into the dark, bursting with pride.

My last thought before I fell into a dreamless sleep was, *did we really swim all the way to France?* It sounded so crazy; I could barely believe it was true. The only thing I *was* sure about was that I'd shared a very special day with some truly amazing people. Mostly my swim teammates, but also the invaluable boat crew. I knew for certain that I would never forget what we had been through together. Not for the rest of my life.

And I haven't forgotten it, and neither has Sandra, BC and Coxy. We are all still close friends but more than that, we have an unbreakable bond. Sometimes, when I'm talking about leadership, I think back to my first hour in the water of that swim. I had put the team together, knowing that I was the weakest swimmer. I also knew that the team was stronger because I was in it. Leadership is not about being able to do everything yourself, or about being the best at it, it's about assembling a team that together becomes greater than the sum of its parts.

CHAPTER 10
LEARNING BY MAKING MISTAKES

L essons in leadership come at us right, left and centre throughout our lives, whatever we do and wherever we are. Luckily, we don't all aspire to be leaders, but I'm pretty certain we all want to be led by competent ones. If we're lucky, we get leaders who help us to live better lives, inspire us to reach our potential and ensure we value things that help everyone, not just ourselves.

Leadership Wisdom

Watch, listen, learn and be the best leader you can be.

Leading the English Channel swim team was a quantum leap in my leadership journey. One of the light bulb moments for me was how I felt about leading the team. I have always had a tendency to suffer from 'imposter syndrome', always waiting for someone to call me out for what I don't know. That swim taught me about my strengths and weaknesses, and allowed me to value what I bring to a team as the leader. I knew what I could and what I couldn't do, and it reinforced one of my strengths, which is when I do something, I'm all in. I want to hold on to it and give it everything, whatever it is. If I decide to do something, look out because I'm all in!

Leadership Wisdom

Listen and learn, learn, learn.

In my business life at that time, I was running a successful consultancy working with some very successful businesses. I was leading a group of experienced consultants, placing them with businesses to improve their sales functions and helping them grow. My experiences during the swim and what it taught me about myself led to a significant change in how I wanted my business to evolve. My confidence was high, and I was full of energy and a new self-awareness. It enabled me to embark on an ambitious plan.

Winston Churchill summed it up perfectly when he said: "Continuous effort, not strength or intelligence, is the key to unlocking our potential."

I have found this to be true for successfully completing the Channel swim, rowing three thousand miles across the Atlantic from La Gomera to Antigua, growing and being innovative in my business life. When I think of continuous effort, I get a mental picture of our family dog, Nala, with a bone. She doesn't need strength or intelligence; she just applies herself to the task of getting all the tasty goodness from it.

This is even more pertinent when I think about leadership. Good leadership requires continuous effort. I fully believe leading by example is by far the most successful way to motivate and inspire a team to give their best effort. But, leading by example is about the application of effort, not being the best at the task. In the Channel swim, I wasn't the strongest swimmer, and I don't think I was the most mentally prepared either, but as leader, throughout the significant challenge, I demonstrated a concerted and continuous effort to overcome my self-doubt and less than perfect swimming technique to set a good pace and be present for everyone. It took a huge amount of effort to keep going, leading by example and showing the team that putting in the hard work would bring the result we all wanted.

Leadership Wisdom

Leadership is not about being the best, it's about continuous effort to ensure the team have what they need to succeed.

I absolutely don't believe that leaders are born. I certainly wasn't. They might be allocated leadership at a young age, volunteer, or sometimes be given the role by default. Leading a team involves a diverse range of skills, and it's a tough ask for anyone to have the full set of strategic, diplomatic, business and people skills needed to be effective without significant experience and training.

As my consultancy business grew, I realised I would never be able to reach enough of the businesses that needed help the most. Businesses that are failing, or not growing, as they need to in order to survive are often unable to hire a consultant or simply don't know who to contact.

I published my first book, *Learning the Ropes,* which outlined my entire sales methodology that, if applied to any business, would help kick start its growth and set it on a path to success. It got great reviews, but I was not satisfied that it hit the spot I was looking for so I decided to create an online platform version with a ready to use Playbook. This is designed to cover every business scenario and is packed with a wealth of knowledge and experience.

As I drilled down into the most common problems businesses face, and through my experience as a consultant working with a variety of businesses, I found that the quick turnover of sales and other staff is one of the most expensive parts of running any business. Furthermore, most of the businesses I worked with needed help because they had ineffective leadership and unmotivated or unsuitable staff.

It set me to thinking about every reason possible for this and the answers were predictable; poor onboarding, poor training and poor recruitment practices. All those business elements fall under the responsibility of the leader. Leading a business, leading a sporting team, directing a play, all require proper attention to three things; vision, people and process. When we think of sporting teams it's obvious that the best people for the positions are selected, they are trained to be the best and they know what their ultimate goal is. We don't even have to think about it, we know it. Directing a play; the director selects the cast, rehearses them, and tells them where to move, what to do and how to do it. Again, it's obvious. Clear leaders and clearly directed teams. We don't have to think about it, we know it.

When I talk about vision, people and process, what I mean is:

- **Vision** - knowing your goal, what you're aiming for, your endgame.
- **People** - working with the right people. People with the skills, training and knowledge to help achieve your

vision. It's worth mentioning that if they don't initially have the skills and knowledge, that's fine, provided they have the commitment and attitude to make it happen.

- **Process** - the methodology and 'how to' that your team uses to achieve your vision.

Leadership positions can command a high salary and rightly so if they are well trained, effective and motivate their team to achieve their potential. But if we expect them to have all the answers without training and clarity of purpose then we will be disappointed.

I published my second book, *Why Do So Many Sales Hires Fail*, to help all those businesses with this problem and don't have the money, time, or access to suitable external help, to highlight the sort of issues that arise and offer solutions to fix them quickly and cost effectively.

CHAPTER 11
AUTHENTICITY IN LEADERSHIP - DOES IT MATTER?

L ife changed during the pandemic and the way we do business changed rapidly and absolutely. When it started we didn't know how it would blow up our lives, take our loved ones and keep us wondering if any of us would even survive. Although it feels like life has resumed, what we think as normal and how we do business, has not.

Leadership Wisdom

Make it your mission to be known as a leader who is humble, honest and authentic.

Due to the proliferation of scandals, the disgraceful behaviour of certain public figures as well as those using the pandemic as a way to get rich quick at the expense of people suffering, we now have less trust in many of our leaders and are more likely to call someone out if we think they're not being truthful.

In addition to that, with the increased use of online platforms and social media being a provider of 'news', it often feels like it's impossible to know what to believe. Add to all that the increasing use of AI material masquerading as human content then can we really trust what we hear, see, and read?

From the minute we wake to the minute we sleep, we're bombarded with noise from social media, emails, ads, and news reporting.

How do we evaluate what's authentic and what's not? What steps can we take to make sure what we're seeing and hearing is true?

The simple answer is we can't. At some point we must decide to believe the people we 'feel' are authentic, because we have no other choice.

As a consultant, speaker and mentor to businesses looking to improve their growth, I'm conscious that sales activity and sales-people are often already near the bottom rung in terms of believ-ability, truthfulness and authenticity.

Leadership Wisdom

When a person is authentic, we're more likely to follow their guidance. Every leader needs to be followed or they're not a leader.

I speak a lot about authenticity because it seems to be vanishing quicker every day. Not only is authenticity at the heart of any good leader, I think it's also at the very heart of being a good person. I know that if I believe a person is authentic, I listen harder, trust what they say and am more likely to follow their guidance. By definition, every leader needs to be followed or, quite simply, they're not a leader.

When I mentor business leaders, I emphasise the importance of clear communication with their staff and customers. Communication is an essential part of building their reputation as a trusted, authentic leader. A good reputation takes time to build and only a second to be destroyed.

We've probably all been guilty of not quite telling the truth, misrepresenting ourselves to get a job, a mortgage, bank loan, or a partner. I know I didn't think twice about it when I was starting out as a naïve teenager in the adult world. At that time, it seemed to me that if it wasn't really hurting anyone, but was getting me what I needed, then it was fine.

Age and experience have taught me that I was wrong, acting this way is never OK, and while it might not have hurt other people, it hurt me. I was not being authentic and while I might have achieved what I wanted, it felt less than it should have. I was building a persona that was not an authentic me and also, the stress of trying to remember what I'd said and to whom was exhausting. How much easier it is to be truthful.

Leadership Wisdom

Authenticity is priceless. It's the best asset a person can have when everyone you know becomes an ambassador for you.

Being authentic made me feel good. I can look at what I've achieved and feel proud of my accomplishments and the great friendships I've built along the way.

A good reputation is the best asset a person can have, it makes ambassadors out of everyone who knows you. Authenticity is the gift that keeps on giving throughout your life. Authenticity is priceless.

Leading by example is a great motivator and good leaders are trained. Whether they're self-taught by hard knocks, learned through experience, as I did, or taught by those who have more formal training, I don't think anyone in any leadership position would be good enough if they believe they're a 'natural leader'. I don't believe any person, in any position, paid or unpaid, can be expected to perform to their potential without appropriate training. Our swim team trained long and hard for our attempt to conquer the English Channel, and our training gave us the confidence to keep going, especially when we realised the enormity of the adventure. I felt the pressure of self-doubt in my leadership ability and drew on every bit of my learning and experience to ensure I could fulfil my position.

All professional team members, in business, sport and the arts, are picked for their good skills and knowledge, but even then, ensuring they continue to grow in expertise means regular training and coaching in the unique environment they've joined. This is also true for leaders. One position leading one team is just the beginning of a leadership journey.

Leadership Wisdom

A good leader understands the people they are leading and has learned what is needed to lead effectively.

Every situation will be different. Every team will be different and complex. Ways of doing things, company knowledge, team knowledge, everything required for a specific new position will involve new strategies being learned and practiced, and will add to existing skills and experience. Good leadership recognises this needs to happen at every level. Being appointed as a leader of any business, sporting team or activity, means learning the ropes and understanding the people to be led as well as what is needed to be effective.

It seems obvious to me that a well-trained team, who know what they're doing, understand what their goal is, who expect to be responsible and held accountable, will outperform any other team. I wonder why it is that we don't seem to demand the same of our leaders.

Surely, a leader who is well trained, well informed and who is able and willing to learn what their team needs to excel, will prosper and be respected. I know from experience that I've had to learn how to motivate teams under me, and have understood how their success is vital to my own individual success. It really matters that leaders understand this.

When I reflect on leadership, especially during the Channel swim and Atlantic row, being authentic meant revealing my vulnerability. I worried that if they saw any chink in my confident armour, the cohesion of the team would be lost and might upset the delicate balance between us. I needed them to believe in my ability to lead them. I wondered what might happen if I revealed any suggestion of what I thought of as weakness. In the middle of nowhere on a tiny boat, I had to share my feelings, it felt even more dangerous not to. What happened? They supported me, understood, reciprocated and it built more trust between us than I could have ever imagined.

I learned a huge lesson, being authentic, and showing vulnerability helped our team grow and deepened the confidence between us. My thorough training in navigation and communication, as well as my years of experience on boats, underpinned my leadership, but it was my willingness to open up to them that was the key strength of our team.

We all felt able to reveal our doubts and fears, our strengths and weaknesses, and it gave us confidence in ourselves and in our team. It gave us a greater understanding, even in the toughest circumstances, that our team would be able to perform under pressure. We had respect and trust in each other. I fully believe that without this two-way communication of trust, the road to success can be difficult, if it's even possible at all.

CHAPTER 12
THE WORLD'S TOUGHEST ROW

W hat on earth was I thinking? I've pondered that question a lot and I still don't have a solid answer. It depends a bit on how I'm feeling, what day it is and whether the sky is blue. What I do know, is that making the decision to do it was not a knee jerk reaction or an idea based on a whim. It came from a deep pit of insecurity about not feeling good enough.

From very early on, I felt the need to validate myself and my place in my family. My parents, and both my brothers, are academics who've all thrived in the classic school, university, career trajectory. I didn't want to fit into any pre-destined path, I wanted something different, I just didn't know what. I have never wanted, and I still don't want, to be put in a box with a neat label.

You might say I had middle-child syndrome. Already not special in any particular way, I was not the oldest, not the baby, just the second, the spare for either of my brothers. Because I rejected the family value of excelling in academia as a measure of self-worth, I've felt like I've been playing catch up ever since leaving school. How could I prove my own value if I didn't perform in the only arena they recognised and understood?

I was always looking for validation, wanting to stand out, wanting to be different. I wasn't an easy kid either, always pushing boundaries, looking for a platform that I could make mine, allowing me to be seen and stand out. All my life, I have never wanted to run with the crowd. I didn't want to fit in or simply disappear as one of many. I wanted to be a major contributor. I still want that. It becomes more important to me the older I get, seeing my own teenagers managing an increasingly difficult world. The less traction I feel I'm getting in my life, the more I look for something extreme to do, to jump-start myself into a positive force for good, leading by example.

I've always looked at extreme events not attempted by many and wondered what is special about those people who do such things? And more importantly to me, do they have something that I don't?

After the Channel swim, I was content for a while, buoyed and satisfied. I'd proven myself able to succeed in something huge, settled down and forged ahead with my business, published my first book and things were going well. That is until the swim started to feel like a long time ago and the nagging voice telling me I wasn't good enough started piping up again.

That conversation with my Dad, when I put into words something I'd only been half-heartedly considering, was the moment it became real. I hadn't told anyone, not my wife, not my kids, I hadn't a clue who might do it with me, but casually mentioning it aloud to my Dad set it in motion. In that moment of madness, when I wanted my Dad to be proud of me, my fate was sealed and the idea of the Atlantic row took hold.

Leadership Wisdom

Don't put off the tough conversations. As leader, it's your responsibility to ensure the success of the team and this can only be achieved if everyone is committed to the team goal.

The enormity of what I was planning started to hit home. After telling my family of my intentions, while thinking in the back of my mind it wasn't possible, I had to face the huge first hurdle: choosing my teammates. I approached Neil, and, great guy that he is, he said *yes* immediately, but then we were almost three years out from the start date so perhaps we both felt blasé about it. After all, we had literally years to prepare, two other team-mates to recruit and plenty of time. Getting Woolley to agree was so easy! He jumped at the opportunity and I wondered from the outset if, like me, he had demons of his own to silence. It was harder for him because he lived further away so it was not as easy for him to train with Neil and me, but he never wavered in his commitment and was a solid member of our crew from the start.

We had a fourth member of our crew, but after a year he fell by the wayside, the pressure of life, work and a young family taking precedence over an adventure. It was a very tough decision to let him go, but in business I had learned that lesson the hard way. If you're going to have the tough conversation then don't put it off as getting it over with is better for you, better for the team and certainly better for the person involved. So, with only 12 months to go, we changed our status to row as a three and 'The World's Toughest Row' just got a little tougher.

Neil and I trained together, rowing on our own little stretch of the English Channel in Seaford. I knew, from our first time out, that Neil was a stronger and tougher rower than I was and in the early days I tried hard keeping up with his pace. His superior strength and ability meant that he was powering on and I was struggling to keep up. That annoying voice in my head returned, whispering that I wasn't good enough. Over the next year we all trained every day on our rowing machines and built up our fitness by walking and cycling. We also attended all the mandated courses for navigation, safety and race protocols.

It was clear from the start that I'd be the one in charge of navigation, using the technology in the boat, as neither Neil nor Woolley really wanted to learn how to use it. Now that I look back on it, this was not a wise decision. We should all have been fully proficient with every onboard procedure, and I think in hindsight it was a measure of how much we were focusing on the physical endurance rather than the overall experience and what we needed to do to get from La Gomera to Antigua while battling tides and winds and everything else the Atlantic might throw at us.

Leadership Wisdom

Insist on proper training and cross training in all important matters. Plan for extreme circumstances with built-in procedures for any emergency.

After months of training, raising money for our two charities, securing sponsors, getting our personal lives in order just in case...the day arrived for us to leave for the final race preparations. It was both massively exciting and terrifying, and I felt ready and yet, not ready. I'd always looked at the ocean row as something I wondered if I could do – what would it feel like, could I do it and what did I need to be capable of to be successful? Now the moment of truth was here, and I was going to find out. I had doubts about my fitness. Would I be able to keep up with the continuous effort of the rowing? How would I cope with blisters on my hands and arse? We'd seen some pretty horrible images in our training events and they haunted me.

It was good to get to La Gomera and immerse ourselves into the full race culture, and I was able to push my anxiety deep down and focus on everything around me; the other boats, the officials, the hugely professional organisation, Atlantic Campaigns, that creates such a safe and spectacular event. The atmosphere was amazing, the selection of people from different countries, all ages and sizes, men and women intent on not only completing but enjoying this mammoth physical and mental endurance event.

Neil, Woolley and I, Team Ocean Dadventure, made our final preparations, underwent inspections and passed all the testing that marked us as fit to start. It was exciting to be in the final countdown to the start of our great adventure.

RACE DAY - THE START

Sam had flown out to join me the night before we left. It was a complete surprise and although it was wonderful, it also threw me a bit, taking me right back to the feeling of reckless abandonment of my family. My wife, my son and daughter, and all the what ifs I couldn't think about.

That morning I barely ate breakfast as I needed to focus and get my head in the game. There were so many people standing above the boardwalk and I knew Sam was amongst them but I didn't want to catch her eye, I needed to let go. The thought nagged at me that if I saw her, it would make the ordeal I was putting her and the kids through too real, and while I wanted with all my heart to be there for them, I also knew that I wanted to do this. Had to do this.

I forced myself to focus and with Neil and Woolley beside me, I let myself settle properly into our team. By the time the Race Director shook our hands before we stepped into our boat, all I could feel was excitement. We were ready, the sun was shining, the sky was a brilliant blue and the sound of people, the splashing of oars in the water, the feel of the ocean already under us, brought everything to a moment of absolute clarity.

We had done it; three years of preparation and hard graft had led us to this moment. It was happening. This tiny boat was where we would live until we hit land in Antigua 3000 miles across a wild ocean. We all felt the excitement, the moment upon us that we had stepped into the unknown with no idea how we would react over the long days and nights to come.

Neil and Woolley took their seats to row us away from the jetty and I stood and navigated out of the harbour. It was daunting, it was scary, my heart was racing, and the thought that I might not come back crossed my mind. Doubt crept in, but seeing Neil and Woolley rowing and the people quickly disappearing as we left the safety of the harbour, I pushed it away. I had never vocalised to Sam, or Neil and Woolley, that I worried that we might not make it, and I think that was the right thing to do.

As the skipper of Ocean Dadventure, I felt a responsibility to Neil and Woolley. Throughout the entirety of the voyage, it never left me, and at times the feeling of it became overwhelming.

I kept a daily video diary and upon reviewing it after our return, I realised how much I had censored what I was feeling. I would record my daily update on my phone but quickly realised that on such a small boat, I would be overheard. This pretty much rendered it useless as a personal log because it was sanitised to the max.

MY DAILY DIARY (INTERESTING BECAUSE OF WHAT I DON'T SAY)

Day 1: 12 December

Sunny, set off from La Gomera. Looking back at Tenerife, it was a calm night. Realise we need to work out a proper pattern. We were attacked by flying fish, morale is good.

...but what I'm thinking

I can't describe how it feels to leave everyone I love. The thought that I might never see them again overwhelms me. What sort of truly selfish wanker does what I'm doing? And now we're rowing, rowing, just rowing. My shifts came and went during the day and the first night was one of the worst of my whole life.

Day 2: 13 December

We see dolphins and already there is no land in sight. The sea is calm, it's peaceful and I'm very aware of the vastness of the water.

...but what I'm thinking

I know I have the most marine and sea experience, but I'm getting some severe doubts that I'm not tough enough to do this. I'm not the best rower. I know I'm not the best company when things don't go well. Sam has warned them I can be a grouchy sod, but did they believe her and how will it affect them?

Day 3: 14 December

Sound of oars slapping the water emphasises how alone we are, so far away from everything we know and the realisation that we can only go on. There is no turning back.

...but what I'm thinking

It's awkward to wear the harness because it digs into your side. At times, we've all forgotten to clip in when we've had to get up from a rest to help turn the boat when a wave has pushed us beyond the safety margin of the autopilot. In the rush, typically when it's rough, it can be minutes before you realise you've forgotten to clip on. When you do, a wash of fear and dread consumes you with what might have happened. In rough seas there would be zero chance of survival if swept overboard.

Day 5: 16 December

I'm resting in the cabin, laying inside to shield myself from the sun. My beard is growing and I feel we're doing well. There's a good team spirit and we're hoping to pick up the trade winds, which will help our progress. Morale onboard is good. Putting in some hard graft. It's windy at night, hot and sunny during the day. On the whole, very pleased.

...but what I'm thinking

1-hour rowing rotations now, with 2 hours rest, rowing as a single at night. I pressed play as the sun went down and the first track was *How Do I Say Goodbye* by Dean Lewis. That was it. I hardly slept when I was off shift through doubt, sadness and missing my family so much it felt like my heart was breaking in my chest.

Day 6: 17 December

It was an emotional night; a special song came on the playlist and I was suddenly in floods of tears. All positive though, just a reminder of home and how far away we are. Wearing jackets at night as it's cold and vast in the dark.

Day 7: 18 December

The snack swaps have already started. I traded a pack of wine gums for our last orange. Being at sea made me think of the sailors of old dying from scurvy. The orange was a real treat, actual food, smelled divine, a taste of home.

Day 8: 19 December

Rowing with dolphins, they really are the Labradors of the ocean. Made me feel happy and safe seeing them so at home playing in the water. They swim along with us, making me feel like they're urging us on.

...but what I'm thinking

Earlier in my life I had an accident with a glass milk bottle and needed 63 stitches in my left hand. I am lucky to have full use of it, though it added to my anxiety about the battering my hands were taking from rowing. My hands felt hot and then became red raw, then they scabbed and split. The pain was excruciating. Over the weeks they calloused, which reduced the pain.

Day 9: 20 December

Woke at dawn, the sea is choppy and the wind is fierce.

Day 14: 25 December

Christmas Day, we put on party hats and grinned for a photo in the sunshine.

Day 16: 27 December

Drifting, we go beam on and had to work to right the boat. It's hard work and not without risk, but we managed it. When I woke up after my rostered sleep, we'd made 22 miles. Still dark at 7:30 am. Windy and trying to make up the pace. The forecast is rough until Friday. Neil's birthday, we raise our water bottles to him.

Day 17: 28 December

Sunburnt. Struggling with the northerly winds. It's been a battle since Christmas Day. We've had 30,40,50-foot swells behind us. We hear on the sat phone that other boats have capsized. We're laying up, beam on. This is a good boat, but we are hot and sweaty in the cabins.

Neil is feeling claustrophobic and needs one of the cabins just for him. This means that I am always going to share with Woolley who is a big bloke and it's a tight squeeze. We're all finding the food awful now and are feeling out of sorts. Can't wait for the wind to turn and we're all looking forward to jumping in the water when it's calmer.

...but what I'm thinking

The days were hot and the sweat rolled down between my shoulder blades and into my shorts and arse crack. The constant, repetitive rowing movement creates sores that, for the first few weeks, we all suffered from. I was forced to rest face down with Sudacream splattered all over my arse like a baby to help the sores heal. Eventually, they scabbed over and fell off. My shorts were littered with bits of skin for days. Horrible.

Day 18: 29 December

The forecast is better but last night was the worst so far. Neil is struggling with his claustrophobia and Woolley suffered a panic attack.

At 6 am I had to lay on the deck to rest, too close for two in the cabin. We're battling the weather and all struggling emotionally. We're all feeing gloomy, and I took five washes over the side during my shift. I got soaked. This has become a crisis management point because it takes about 15 minutes to strip off, get dry, set wet clothes to dry and then try to catch some sleep before the next shift. Everywhere feels damp and I can't sleep in wet clothes because it gets too cold.

...but what I'm thinking

The sea life is incredible. Our first couple of nights we were visited by two massive pods of dolphins jumping and playing near the boat. They are beautiful creatures, a magical sight. They boost our spirits when we're feeling low, and we need them today as we're all feeling down and damp with a long way to go.

Day 19: 30 December

Today was a good day, woke up and moved away from the stormy weather but it was tough rowing, not much swell, no wind, like rowing through concrete. Not much wildlife, some flying fish but not much else. It feels like we're very alone out here. We're all hoping for calm tomorrow so we can jump in the water and clean ourselves. The bottom of the boat also needs cleaning as I'm getting concerned about what barnacles and seaweed might be caught on the bottom, slowing us down. This has been one of our best days so far, the emotional lows we were all feeling seem to be settling down again.

1896 Miles to Antigua.

Day 20: 31 December

Last night was tough and we all struggled. The rowing was very hard work and the sun came up, which felt hot and bright early on. It was the perfect day to enter the water. We jumped over the side to cool off and, as suspected, the bottom of the boat was covered in weeds, algae and stuff growing. Woolley cleaned it all off and our speed increased from one knot to four, which was an incredible transformation. We did our washing and Woolley prepared dinner as the sun was setting.

Saturday is our treat day; we have chocolate and a can of fizzy drink. We all agreed this was our best day so far. We're all feeling good and the boat feels great. Tomorrow there is more breeze forecast, which is good. We're in a much better place than we were a week ago.

...but what I'm thinking

It's been a full three weeks for the conditions to be safe enough for us to enter the water. I've often felt irrationally annoyed because we're not making the progress I'd like, and can hear Sam in my head warning the guys that I'm not at my best when I'm tired. Understatement of the year! My bad temper evaporated when Woolley did such an amazing job of clearing nearly two inches of weed and ocean gunk off the bottom of the boat. I was glad I had been able to shield them from my horrible mood.

Day 21: 1 January

New Year's Day, up on deck at 7 am, put loads of miles in today. Saw another boat, a New Zealand pair. Our rowing shifts were fast, averaging three knots. Feeling a little bit low and shared how I was feeling with the others. We're not even halfway yet and it feels like there's a very long way to go. We need more music as we've been through the playlist at least four times already. In the cabin, I checked our instruments and am pleased to see we have travelled 100 miles in two days. We are 1,892 miles to Antigua. The food tastes absolutely dreadful, I can hardly bear to eat it. We have all identified the packs we know we're never going to eat.

Day 22: 2 January

We're into week four and have favourable winds but still such a long way to go.

Day 23: 3 January

Made good mileage, 65 miles of hard work. We had a following wind, not much wildlife and we miss them when they're not around. Kite birds, small and acrobatic, kept us company for a while. We all put our heads down and focused on our rowing.

...but what I'm thinking

Rowing 12 hours a day is tough, so tough I can't actually describe it. If you told any sane person that you planned to row for 12 hours a day for 7 weeks, non-stop, I'm pretty sure they'd say it was utter madness, and it is.

Day 24: 4 January

Very windy today, we have heavy following seas and it's very choppy. Another relentless heads down rowing day. Our daylight shift pattern was one hour on, one hour off with two rowers on, one resting. Rotating through. At night, we generally only had one rower for each hour, and two rowers resting, so that we could stretch the night rests to two hours.

Day 25: 5 January (Morning)

We had a good night, drifted a bit but a good wind behind, gusting at about 25 knots. Difficult to get into a rhythm rowing because the oars get snatched and canon back to hurt your mid-section, which takes the wind right out of you and has the potential to do real damage.

Our position in the race has dropped back, several boats are on a better course and have moved up. Despite that, our progress is going well and we're in good shape. As the navigator, I'm keeping an anxious eye on our heading as we mustn't drop too far south or it'll be hard work tracking back up and waste our energy. We're close to the halfway mark, the weather is windy and the sun is shining.

...but what I'm thinking

As skipper, the stress is building. Every shift I have to check the instruments to make sure we're still on course as agreed with Tim, our weather router. I would call him most days to confirm our course for the next 24 hours as it would add days to our journey if we drifted unchecked. Really, though, all I wanted was to hear a voice to connect with civilisation. It helped me feel less alone.

Day 25: 5 January (Evening)

We've had a very good day. Following seas, 30-foot swells and relentless rowing. Our average speed has been three knots but getting up to eight knots with the wind and tide assists. We're all feeling comfortably uncomfortable. Itching to clean the boat again to get rid of algae and barnacles, primarily to help us increase our speed through the water but we first have to wait for much calmer seas and we're all feeling very tired. Waves knocked me off the rowing seat today and I got swiped by the oars in the ribs and shins. We're facing many challenges in the boat and tomorrow we'll be happy to cross the halfway mark. At 25 days completed, we're averaging 60 miles a day.

Day 26: 6 January

We're now officially at the halfway point with 1581 miles still to go! Feeling positive having past this significant milestone.

Day 27: 7 January

Good progress overnight, although not much rowing. We've put on 72 miles and there've been some huge waves and winds at 30 knots. We have relentless following seas and there's not much we can do in these conditions. It accentuates how small we are, how vast the ocean is and the incredible power of nature.

One of the oars got stuck under the boat and snapped in the big swell. It was a scary moment as the waves broke over the top of us. We exchanged our first heated words and our tempers flared as fear, pent up petty niggles and the relief that no one was hurt, or worse, washed over us as fierce as the seas that had us in their grip.

It's Saturday so knowing it was treat day helped us recover from our emotional outburst.

…but what I'm thinking

I was having a bad day and it's so very tough. I had strong words with the guys, we were all on edge. It doesn't happen very often. I sat and suffered in silence, wishing so hard that I was anywhere but on that tiny bloody boat miles from anywhere. The tinted glasses came out to hide my tears as I tried to return to an even keel.

Day 29: 9 January

Yesterday was windy and tiring, and I'm too exhausted to even post an update. We have travelled a good distance, putting on 89 miles, and 79 miles each day. We now have under 1400 to go but that still seems like a daunting amount. I'm now trying to eat the muesli with cold water as eating is becoming increasingly terrible. The music is good and keeps us going, and our camaraderie has recovered its equilibrium. I have my private beefs and sometimes keeping this video diary is difficult because I feel I have to censor what I say. Something I've heard Neil say many times is, "be kind."

We're still moving too fast for it to be safe to clean the bottom of the boat. We're grinding it out but sometimes, during the night-shift if the weather's not too bad, it's relaxing looking out at the moonlight across the vastness of the ocean. Listening to audiobooks and getting into a rhythm with my strokes, whole minutes go by when I don't want to check my watch to see how much longer I have left to row until my shift ends. Looking at the moonlight makes me think about what changes I'm going to make to my life when I return.

Our expected arrival time has been brought forward thanks to our great progress over the past few days. Our speed is averaging three knots and things are running pretty smoothly, so much better than our first two weeks when we were all pretty scared. We were all covered in bruises from getting knocked off our rowing seats and Woolley got swamped with water when he'd just left the cabin.

…but what I'm thinking

The night shifts are absolute torture, and none of us wants to row, but we all know we can't just pause and lose that much time. When it's your turn you have to get on deck and put in the shift. There is no snoozing the alarm, that's a luxury we don't have. When I was counting down seconds waiting for the next rower to take over, I started getting angry expecting them to be late. Even an extra minute felt inexcusable.

Day 30: 10 January

Good day today. Got up early and it still looked too rough to risk cleaning the boat, but Woolley decided to do it anyway. He never missed an opportunity to get in the water, but it was so refreshing, who could blame him. He jumped in and did a great job. There's not as much to clear off as last time, but although it's been slow going, we've now picked up the pace a bit.

Saw some sea birds today, a tuna and the usual flying fish that often land on the boat. It's best to duck if you spot one coming, but you rarely do. Mostly they come at night and they come so fast, causing a bruise if you catch one on the body or face. We always carefully pick them up and chuck them back into the water alive. We're all feeling tired but working well as a team. We've fallen into roles, which works efficiently. I am the skipper and navigator; I operate all the instruments and communicate with other vessels if needed. Woolley is the head chef and water manager, and Neil is the engine room and anchor for our rowing effort. We've nicknamed him Diesel because he is strong, reliable and all round awesome (oarsome)! We're grateful to have such an amazing, well-designed boat, and at this point, while everything is working well and we're in a good place, we can't wait for it to be over.

We were discussing whether we'd do this again? I said an emphatic *no*, as I'd promised my wife that even if I was tempted, I wouldn't. Asked if I did, who would I do it with? I said I couldn't imagine doing it with anyone else. We feel like a team, settled in our roles, coping with the difficulties, but if I think about why and who, I doubt if any of the other teams are doing as well as us.

I remember a conversation with our safety officer, Ian Couch, who told me that it's not unusual for teams to arrive in Antigua and never speak to each other again, ever. At the time, it was hard for me to imagine, but after 30 days, I understand it. I don't think it will happen to us, but we've still quite a way to go.

…but what I'm thinking

For the most part, there isn't time to think, which I know sounds ridiculous. Often, we'd chat about something and that would become the topic of the day. As we were three blokes around age 50, we had all sorts of chats about life, children and partners, which was fun and actually quite revealing, and established a closeness and deep level of trust between us. Some juicy bits? Sorry, Chatham House rules. Suffice to say, we're all pretty similar, we all have a shit load of personal baggage.

Day 31: 11 January

Another tough day, huge swells, very stressful. The boat's been smashed by waves travelling up to 10 knots. Feels very out of control. Overtook a solo rower and saw a tuna jump out of the water. Now we're clicking along at 3.5 knots, and I've estimated we need to row 70 miles a day to reach Antigua to meet my 50-day target. It's tough, relentless, but we're sticking to it and doing well.

Day 32: 12 January

Back in the cabin after a very long day. It's now a calendar month since we set off. We did OK overnight, but the batteries are low, which is a minor crisis because we need our power for the navigation, communication and desalinating the water. We should have enough water to see us through until the batteries are recharged.

We have just under 1200 miles to go, tracking at 70 miles a day now. We found water in the cabin, though not much, and we think it came from the clothing and wet shoes. An oar was lost overboard when it broke through the rowing gate and now we're down to only one spare.

I have boils on my arse so the rowing seat hurts and my hands are also in pain. We saw sharks today so we're hoping they're not circling and sizing us up for their next meal. There were also three or four dolphins swimming alongside, checking us out. All in all, today finished well, despite a few early setbacks.

...but what I'm thinking

During the night shift I'd count around 15 songs before I could return to the cabin and rest, my body hurting all over. After two songs, every part of me was crying out to stop, unable to imagine how I'd get through the shift. I thought about my Dad how I always wanted to make him proud trying to compensate for my lack of academic success. I know it sounds crazy, but it's always been a mental drain for me. Being asked to leave home at 16 because I dropped out of school has left me with deep scars and hang-ups.

Day 33: 13 January

Today was a struggle. I've calculated we need to increase our daily rate to 83 miles to meet our arrival target, which feels like a huge ask, essentially achieving nearly 20% more than our current rate. It was a tough day on the oars, which again felt like rowing through concrete. We kept bumping into metres long stretches of seaweed. I also had a tight hamstring and had to rest. Physically, I feel like I'm starting to fall apart with all the bits that are starting to hurt. Two buckets of freshly desalinated water were knocked over while washing. The batteries are topped up though. Many flying fish landed on the deck. We try to avoid them hitting us and then throw them back in. Today was slow and hard, which felt like a kick in the guts when we need to up the pace. We're all at a low point, desperate to reach the end and see our families. We know we have to work hard and although we're struggling, team morale is high.

Day 34: 14 January

A better day today. The wind was in the right direction and helped our progress, though we're still bothered by clumps of floating seaweed hampering our effort and there's not much wildlife around. It was a clear night with so many stars. The non-stop rowing is getting more and more difficult. This afternoon was hot but we were able to wash in the water and clean the bottom of the boat again.

We're hoping to reach the final 1000 miles by tomorrow. We saw on the satellite that the first boat has already reached Antigua. Despite being a bit envious, we're happy with our progress. I'm managing to eat a bit more, I'm not sure why, perhaps I've just got used to the completely tasteless and horrible unnatural texture of the freeze-dried food that turns to gluggy mush when it's reconstituted.

…but what I'm thinking

My emotions are all over the place. One moment I was singing along, marvelling at the sunrise and then a song comes on that reminds me of my Dad and I'm over-whelmed and in floods of tears.

Day 35: 15 January

I woke to a beautiful sunrise with exactly 1000 miles to go, so it's not all doom and gloom, even when we had a massive rain shower. We're all doing well.

Day 36: 16 January

Still pitch black at 8 am, an uncomfortable night and everything's damp. We've found water in the front and back cabins, more than we feel comfortable with and have decided to clean everything out.

The challenges are so much more than just the relentless nature of the rowing. It was a good day, though, even when I was in the front cabin and a wave slammed into the back, spinning us 180 degrees. Felt very nervous going to sleep and then in the middle of the night, we were turned beam on and felt water in the back cabin. First thought was that we're sinking as three quarters of an inch seems too much for condensation and damp. Everything smelled of mildew and mould so we drained it out and smothered everything in disinfectant. It was heavy going, long day on the oars not helped by each of us trying to process our general anxiety.

Our progress was disappointing, only 37 miles in 12 hours, which means we're falling way behind what we want to achieve. We've started getting messages from people on Instagram, which brings us an incredible boost. We're now 912 miles from Antigua.

...but what I'm thinking

Another day when I just feel angry, shouting into the waves towards my Dad. "If this isn't good enough for you, then I don't give a fuck." Is this, after all, just a vain attempt to impress my late Dad?

Day 37: 17 January

Another tough day, not much wind and the rowing was difficult. We only achieved 62 miles in 24 hours. We're all disappointed. It's very hot and it's a chore to get on the oars. My hands are covered in blisters. In fact, I now have blisters on my blisters, my hands are a painful mess.

We didn't see any wildlife, which always makes it more difficult, and neither did we sight other boats. Just endless ocean. The food, surprisingly, is going down better and I'm certain my brain has accepted there's no choice but to eat whatever is available. We've almost run out of tea bags, chocolate and biscuits, which is very depressing. Our families are due to fly out to Antigua and there should only be eleven more nights until we see land. Tomorrow, we're hoping to pick up some helpful winds to speed us to our destination.

Day 38: 18 January

A very hard day. 36 miles. Nowhere near enough. Neil fell off the toilet bucket, which just about summed up how we were all feeling, but we all had a good laugh anyway. With less than 800 miles to go, we saw a curious whale down one side of the boat. Magnificent creatures but a little alarming to realise just a little nudge and this powerful body would make mincemeat of our boat.

After a bad night we were all out on deck having a few cross words as we're all feeling under pressure and frustrated at our lack of progress. The wind and current is against us. A bird that's been following us for a while came and nestled on the boat. Bad news; we're now running low on coffee.

Day 39: 19 January

Yesterday was the lowest I've felt on the trip after looking at the distance we still need to cover and wishing for the first time I wasn't on this fucking boat. Wearing my sunglasses to hide my tears and couldn't get the negativity out of my head. Determined to feel better, I put some music on the speaker and forced myself to return to a positive mindset.

...but what I'm thinking

I'm so angry and there's no reason for it. I found myself shouting into the wind and out to the ocean, "is that all you've fucking got? That ain't stopping us!"

Day 40: 20 January

We were able to regroup today and after discussing it, agreed to a new strategy. We won't look further than the day. We've less than 700 miles to go. Unfortunately, the little bird that had nestled on the boat flew away but we think it dropped into the water and died, which was a deeply upsetting moment. It reminded us of the power of nature and how small and insignificant we are. In the distance we saw a container ship on a collision course with us. I contacted the captain just to be safe, but they had already seen us on their AIS, so all was well. Food is definitely more palatable. We're rowing hard and need to check the bottom of the boat again.

Day 41: 21 January

Less than 650 miles to go; there's one more day of coffee remaining, and one piece of chocolate and one biscuit each per day. We're all looking forward to seeing our families. We're making good progress but need to adjust our course in a northerly direction to hit Antigua as we've drifted a bit far to the south. To change direction, we're battling to row an hour on, half off.

The winds are to the Northeast and it was an uncomfortable night. We're working well as a team with a single aim, but a couple of days have been added to our arrival time, which is disappointing, and our families have had to rearrange their flights and accommodation. Our new ETA is a week on Monday, putting us in Antigua on 29th January.

At night, we're trying to rest in intervals of one hour on, half off, but it's spooky at night. Blowholes from nearby whales make us nervous as they're dangerously close to the boat. We managed to get a wind behind us and put in a lot of hard work. In the morning, we saw a pod of about 20 dolphins. The water was blue and crystal clear.

...but what I'm thinking

The day shifts can be horrible. They are long and relentless. Woolley isn't the most proficient or consistent rower, which at first I resented, but I have come to be incredibly grateful that he manages the cooking, cleaning, solar battery replenishment and desalinating our water. His attention to these vital tasks has meant I can trust him and focus on our navigational needs, keeping us on course. Sometimes I had wished the guys were able to share the navigation duties, especially today when we drifted off our course, but each having our own area of responsibility has made us a great and equal team, each playing to our strengths.

Day 42: 22 January

8 am after a good nightshift, we're rowing to the north of Antigua but Ian, the safety officer, has advised us to maintain our course and then on Sunday and Monday we can shape up to Antigua. We still have 500 miles to go, supported by whales and dolphins obviously curious at what we're doing in their back-yard. We jumped in the water; the boat was clean, and it was refreshing to change clothes. There is no coffee left, only ration packs. We have a reasonably tough day ahead but we're all feeling better after the bad days we endured over the last week.

...but what I'm thinking

I remember the first time Woolley and I jumped in with our harnesses and extra rope. I looked down into the dark blue abyss below and thought *Fuck! That's three miles down to the seabed. If anything happens to me right now, I'm gone.* After the initial adrenaline rush of fear, it reminded me how small and insignificant we are. Literally, just a drop in the ocean. We always struggled to get back in the boat after cleaning it. Even in calm water, it was awkward climbing back onboard. Again, I thought, if any of us fell in, especially in rough weather, we'd never make it back. It's a sobering thought that's never far away.

Day 43: 23 January

Load of flying fish, coming in like missiles. We're rowing hard and all tired. We've now adjusted to the finishing route with 440 miles to go. Hoping we're going to meet our revised ETA, which means only six more days remaining. We're beam on to the swell and wind, which is pushing us along. The challenge is to keep going or we'll find ourselves going backwards. I'm really struggling with cramping.

Day 44: 24 January

393 miles to Antigua. We covered 68 miles yesterday and maintaining our course. The barnacles are now fixed but I worry I'm not pulling my weight with my hamstrings hampering my progress. We're still plagued by flying fish, but all feel a moral responsibility to scoop them safely back into the ocean. It's early morning and even though we worked hard, we still only managed 70 miles, which is disappointing. We're pushing ourselves very hard and we're all extremely tired. The whales and dolphins have left us.

...but what I'm thinking

I've always had a dodgy right hamstring ever since sustaining a rugby injury, which repaired enough to continue playing but I've always been careful and worried about it, and it was always on my mind whilst training for this. At various times, I've found myself shuffling onto one cheek more than the other to protect it. I haven't shared it with the others much, but now I'm constantly in pain from the cramping and having to press on regardless.

Day 45: 25 January

266 miles to go, a tough night, very hard work. We're all totally focussed. There was a north-easterly roll and no traction. Feeling very pissed off. A lot of hard work, hour on, 30 minutes off, very tough. We've been doing this punishing schedule for 2 days non-stop just to get further north. The team is working well together but we're all starting to get jealous as we see other teams finishing. Our friends and families are now in Antigua, anxiously awaiting our arrival at the finish line.

...but what I'm thinking

Before leaving for La Gomera, I'd often thought about how I would ever be able to look Madeleine or Caroline in the eye if something happened to Neil or Woolley. I never shared this anxiety with anyone, but it was always there. Now we are so close the burden feels heavier than ever. We are all struggling and just want to reach the end. I'm weighed down by the knowledge that I'm the one responsible for the way they're feeling as it was me who asked these guys to join me.

Day 46: 26 January

We only completed 46 miles yesterday. There were a lot of floating weeds and a slow wind that suddenly changed to full northerly, and we had to drop the power anchor to avoid being swept off course. A residual swell is slowing our progress.

Day 47: 27 January

Yesterday we were all very low and despondent. Rowing through treacle. But woke this morning with only 161 miles to go. We're happy because we might beat a boat that was due to arrive before us. We're now in sight of the finish line and it's a great feeling.

...but what I'm thinking

Now we're in sight of the finish, I'm no longer shouting into the wind, having made peace with my emotions. Years of thinking I wasn't good enough, and being hurt by the feeling my parents weren't proud of me, were simply wrong. I've come to realise, and I know deep down, that they've always loved me. I know my Dad was proud of me. How am I only just now understanding it? Did it take 7 weeks on the ocean to bang it into my stubborn head? To know that as a gobby 16-year-old, my folks didn't know how to deal with me, and I don't suppose I knew how to deal with them either. Mountain; meet immovable object.

Day 48: 28 January

Feeling emotional. We had a good day and a good night. We are getting more messages of support including one from Joe Marler, who is an England rugby player, and one from Kevin Sinfield, England rugby coach, which was a real thrill. We've only got 100 miles left and have received the initial instructions for our arrival. It's all becoming very real! We are now busting our arses to get into the harbour as soon as we can. We're all in floods of tears, laughing, just very emotional; three tired, bearded, muscle-bound rowers, what a hilarious sight we'd be, but happily we're still too far out to be snapped on a stray camera!

Day 49: 29 January

LAST DAY! It's here. We now have less than 50 miles left and we've decided to push ourselves really hard for this final day and make it to the harbour as soon as we possibly can. As we made our final approaches, we were all complaining about how disgusting, sweaty and dirty we were but then, out of nowhere, it started raining. Proper torrential 'fat' rain. We stripped off, soaped up and showered before spending the afternoon chatting and listening to music while we prepped for our arrival.

Once across the finish line, we brought out the flares as the media took photos, all that official stuff. When we finally stepped off the boat, our sea legs had us wobbling all over, though luckily our families were there to catch and wrap us in hugs.

It was a perfect evening, warm, a slight breeze and a thousand stars. It felt like home.

…but what I'm thinking

There were many times when I felt we could have rowed better and more in sync. I could've raised it with the guys, but my decision as skipper was that a happy boat is more likely to get us safely to our destination. I am leading a team that gels well, and we all have the same common objective of rowing our boat safely home. End of!

I've told the guys that I will not step off the boat until they are safely ashore. It will be my last responsibility as their skipper and I know I will feel full of emotion, not least, because we are all alive at the end of this incredible adventure.

CHAPTER 13
WAS I A GOOD SKIPPER?

I t didn't take me long to start thinking about what I could have done better. I reflected on my video diary and, as I said, realised how much I'd censored my thoughts as I was always conscious that, even alone in the cabin where I recorded my diary, I could easily be overheard. I couldn't get rid of the things that were starting to niggle at me. We weren't all equal in our rowing performance and it quickly became apparent that Neil was our linchpin, our anchorman, our outstanding rower. It was his unwavering physical ability that drove our team and we relied on him. In addition to this, Neil was our voice of calm reason. His default reaction is kindness, and it is a superpower that should never be underrated.

As skipper, I constantly felt the heavy responsibility of getting us to the finish line safely. I was always striving to hold my own, worrying that I would let the team down. While I knew I didn't possess the power and physical dominance of Neil, I did feel that being in charge of navigation and communication helped balance things out. Neither Neil nor Woolley wanted to have much to do with that aspect of our journey so they relied on me to keep us on track and to keep us safe, which was fine.

Woolley was not our strongest rower, but he more than compensated by being the ultimate shipmate. He put himself in charge of our meals and other domestic duties. Meal preparation alone was a significant task. All water had to be boiled, added to the freeze-dried packs and then left for 15 minutes before consumption. Three large men each taking care of their own water on a very small boat would have been impossible. Woolley managed this task without any sign of discontent and made sure we had a set dinner time each day. Prepping our meals also cut into his resting periods between shifts. This was an incredible sacrifice because we all valued our precious rest time alone in the cabin, and he would time it so that he would eat his food before taking over the oars while Neil and I ate ours.

Our different abilities and personalities helped us all fill additional roles that made us an amazing team rather than just three rowers.

Leadership Wisdom

In a strong team, addressing petty irritations can do more harm than good. Good leadership requires emotional intelligence and an understanding of human behaviour.

A few times it felt like we were walking on eggshells, each of us harbouring niggles about the others. Should I, as skipper, have insisted on addressing these? Maybe, but I decided that our overall good team spirit could reassert itself, and mostly our niggles against each other were simply symptoms of whatever difficulty we were each coping with emotionally.

A key trigger event for me was the alarm sounding if the boat came off autopilot. As navigator and holding responsibility for our course setting, it was imperative that our autopilot remained on to keep us on the optimum course for our destination. Any deviation could add days to our journey as we would have to fight the weather and ocean currents to get back where we should be. Very early on, the reality of what we were doing hit us hard. The reason 99% of boats that start reach the finish line is that apart from death, sinking or random destruction, there is no other way to stop once you've begun.

The alarm, more often than not, went off at night, and usually when the two not rowing had just got to sleep. The autopilot registers rowing activity, and physical tiredness leads to less careful rowing including the likelihood of flicking the water instead of good drawing strokes. Too many consecutive flicks, or slow oars through the water over a number of minutes is enough to veer off course by the 20 degrees required to trigger the alarm and disengage the autopilot. When this happens, the boat goes beam on, and it's very heavy and hard work fighting the elements to get back on course. One night, we were beam on all night because we were all so spent physically that we couldn't turn the boat round. I was hand steering while Neil and Woolley were both rowing with one arm, but we just couldn't do it.

It always seemed to happen when the weather was squally, with high wind and lashing rain. When the alarm started blaring, we had to get to work immediately. There was no time to put on our waterproofs so, not only did we get soaked, but we also quickly felt cold and struggled to turn the boat while taking in a face full of seawater. Removing our wet clothes afterwards and finding somewhere to leave them to dry was time consuming, and our sleep became very fragmented. Nothing was ever really dry and we were all uncomfortable. Not only that but our skin was often peeling from sunburn, our beards growing wildly, and we generally smelled. Was it any wonder we were irritated by each other?

Leadership Wisdom

Good leadership creates a successful team by solving the issues that cause damaging events without attributing blame.

From a leadership perspective, I had decided that nothing would be gained and potentially our camaraderie could be lost if any of the niggles we felt were aired. I spent many hours going over the different scenarios and wondering how to resolve some of my own issues. I always came back to the understanding that the team is more important than allocating blame in any situation.

I found the rowing shifts so hard; it was relentless with so many miles and so little achieved every day. The level of discomfort was extreme; boils developed on our behinds from poor nourishment and long hours sitting rowing, we all suffered peeling skin from salt and sun damage and we were endlessly tired as the sun during the day was too hot while the nights were too cold, though always conditions were too damp and cramped. Additionally, we all suffered from anxiety and claustrophobia induced by being trapped on a small boat in a vast, unforgiving ocean with no choice but to row ourselves to a safe harbour and home.

Early on, I had rowed too hard, trying to make sure I was pulling my weight, and when the sun was beating down it was easy to become dehydrated and sunburnt. After one particularly long day, I felt completely spent and was burning up from heatstroke, and I could barely stumble from the rowing seat to the cabin. I had been trying too hard to keep up with Neil, who by now we had nicknamed Diesel. I'd got it into my head that as skipper, I should be able to equal his progress, or I'd be letting the team down. Just like those early days of our training on the English

Channel, Neil was able to sprint it, but I wasn't. I was so out of it that the others told me to rest, and they'd take my shifts until I felt rested. I didn't want the others to do my bit and I definitely got the sense that they thought I deserved how I felt for being such an idiot, and they were right. I had been an idiot. In exchange for doing my shifts, and grinning widely, they demanded payment by way of my protein shakes. Hit a man when he's down? I relinquished the protein shakes readily as I felt too rotten to eat or drink anything except water.

The serious nature of what I'd done to the team with my reckless behaviour hit hard. I was annoyed with myself for letting the team down and didn't want the others picking up my slack. I never felt as low as when I wasn't contributing. I was trying too hard to perform at my optimum all the time. I found I was never eating enough because the food was so unpalatable. It was hard to force it down. I was gutted to think they might perceive me to be weak.

Leadership Wisdom

Give members of your team the opportunity to know what you know. Share the knowledge so that in any situation or crisis, there is someone who can step up to lead.

In addition to this, my role as navigator, monitoring the AIS safety equipment that alerted us to any ships or boats in proximity, and managing the communication if we needed to speak to another vessel, meant that if I was out of action, we'd be seriously at risk. I got better, pretty damn quick.

Many times, I recall beginning my shift, particularly at night and being awed by the clear sky and the stars, and after what seemed like hours checking my watch to see it was actually only three minutes into my hour. I would promise myself I wouldn't look again for a long time, but when it seemed like a long time had passed, rowing steadily in the darkness with only my headlamp to tell me I was alive and not dreaming, I would again look at my watch to find only a further two minutes had passed.

Time seemed to have different properties depending on the activity. Rowing a minute was like an hour and resting an hour was like a minute. This time-bending new reality made it hard for me to cope with any kind of timing at all. At night, I would start to feel anxious twenty minutes out from the end of my shift if the light in the cabin didn't turn on at least ten minutes prior to changeover and there was no sound or sight of movement. Whenever that happened, we all began to get annoyed. I couldn't bear someone being even one minute late taking over because it would eat into my rest time that went so quickly and drag out my rowing time that went so slowly.

The rower has to keep rowing or the boat slews around creating a huge problem. This was a persistent problem for me which, looking back on it, was completely irrational and I hope remained unknown to both Neil and Woolley.

Everything was amplified in those conditions and as the skipper, I had to moderate my instinctive reactions and how I communicated. I feel a lot but am able to control my temper without being quick to anger, though on occasions, only a couple, I found myself shouting. The others shouted back and then we quickly lost our appetites for continued hostilities and calmed right down, sorting out whatever had lit our touchpaper like the reasonable people we are.

I did often feel frustrated, though. My experience on boats, my five years on a fishing trawler, owning my own boat that I take on the Channel fishing, has given me a lot of onboard experience and awareness as well as respect for the power of the ocean. This experience found me time and time again, giving guidance about the boat. I knew what knots to use for rope safety and wouldn't let either of them tie their own knots. A reef knot simply is not good enough.

Leadership Wisdom

Insist on comprehensive training, appropriate for the situation or task, particularly when safety is involved. Leave nothing to chance.

It was hard to impress upon them the importance of not wrapping a rope around any part of their body, or not standing in a coil, that the extreme pressure on a rope could kill you in a second. Even the fact that if one of us went overboard, it would likely be impossible for them to be recovered was hard to instil in them.

If you're swept overboard or unintentionally fall over the side without a safety harness clipped in, by the time the boat is turned around and rowed back against the tide, it would likely be too late. That being said, when the ocean was calm and it was possible, we did enter the water, tied securely to the boat, power anchor deployed, to wash and scrape the weed and barnacles that had grown on the bottom of the boat. Woolley wanted to get in the water as much as he could. He loved it and I often stopped him for safety reasons. Neil was quite the opposite and had absolutely no desire to leave the relative safety of the boat.

I was always keeping an eye out for where they were and what they were doing. I had more boat smarts than either of them and a sixth sense about everything happening on board. When I was awake, I was alert and when asleep, I felt like I always had one eye and one ear open.

It was very clear at times like this, when worst case scenarios ran through my mind, that we had never really planned for a crisis situation and it worried me a lot.

Neil and I have known each other a long time, and although we've always been friends, we didn't know each other that well. We respected each other as individuals, and I knew Neil to be thoughtful and kind. Woolley, I didn't know very well at all. He seemed to be a happy-go-lucky sort of person, but I realised pretty quickly that he was very sensitive and not what I originally thought. Neil was the reason there were few occasions when our tempers got the better of us as he was able to influence the conversation or situation away from flare-up points and into safer spaces.

Leadership Wisdom

Even if you're known as a person who 'gets stuff done', don't let that dominate your leadership style. Remember, the team are there for a reason.

I am often described as a person who 'gets stuff done', and it's the phrase most often used when people are asked to describe me. I like it. It sounds strong, focused, and direct. And it is. But it was not what was needed in our team on the boat and for the main event, the rowing, we needed all three of us to get it done.

CHAPTER 14
NIGHT TALK WITH THE STARS

When I first tinkered with the idea of Rowing the Atlantic, I think what I was looking for was an opportunity to feel what it's like to be at the extreme edge of what's possible for me.

How do I get beyond being 'the person who gets stuff done'?

I have always been a control freak. I think it comes from so often feeling out of control in the early part of my life and, being the middle child, I was neither fish nor fowl. I asserted my place by controlling as much as possible and always mistaking that for feeling good enough.

You cannot control everything in the middle of the ocean, knowing that you're only halfway, and realising you just don't want to do it anymore. At times, we'd all had enough. The relentless nature of the rowing, the physical discomfort on so many fronts and the intense claustrophobia of knowing the tiny boat is it. There is literally nowhere to go. But you don't have a choice. There is no option not to do it. There is nothing about it you can control. You can only smile, wave at the dolphins and the flying fish, and keep going.

I have a tattoo on my left shoulder of three stars that represent my wife, Sam, my son, Joseph, and my daughter, Mollie. I had it done whilst training so that, on the journey ahead, I would always have them looking over my shoulder.

After the first few night shifts, I realised that the three stars of Orion's Belt are identical to my tattoo. From that moment on, I always looked forward to my nightly conversations with Sam, Joseph and Mollie.

Night rowing alone is difficult. Unless it's a full moon, there's absolutely nothing to see but darkness all around. However, when you look up and see the magnificence and beauty of the stars above, undiminished by any light pollution, it's the most amazing feeling. We had lamps attached to bands on our heads, but in the dead of night the ocean is full of demons, random splashing, movement and other anomalies that go unnoticed in the glare of the sun.

I looked up to my stars, Orion's Belt, and had the conversation I wished I could have in person. Nothing world shattering, just "how was your day, hope school was good, hope you're looking after Mum." And to Sam, "I'm so proud of you all, how I wish I was with you tonight, are you doing OK?" and "Oh, did I mention, the food is shit and my arse is on fire?"

Talking out loud to the stars, imagining they were my family made me feel less alone. It didn't feel quite so bad, and I didn't feel quite so mad.

THINGS I SHOULD HAVE TAKEN MORE SERIOUSLY AND THE CONVERSATIONS I SHOULD HAVE HAD WITH THE TEAM

I've always had a dodgy right hamstring ever since a rugby injury many years ago. It's one of those injuries that repairs well enough to continue playing but you have to be constantly mindful of it. During our three years of preparation, I had considered it a lot, but now, at night, it became a consistent fear that it might suddenly give way. To protect it, both during preparation and on the ocean, I found myself shuffling onto one cheek more than the other, information I barely shared with the team as though saying it out loud would tempt the ocean gods to strike me down.

Leadership Wisdom

Good leadership demands good communication. Failing to share crucial information can put the team at risk of not being able to achieve their goal.

I had many doubts going into the row, not only about my ability to keep up with the continuous physical effort but also other things like how my arse would cope? We'd all been shown some pretty horrible images in our training events of people with golf ball-sized holes in their butt cheeks where untreated boils had gone septic and created...a crater in the skin.

I wondered how my hands would hold up. I'm not a manual labourer. My work involves a lot of thinking, speaking and using a keyboard. My five years of manual work on a fishing trawler are thirty years in my past and I don't think Woolley has ever done manual work in his life either. I felt totally out of my league with Neil, who has spent his life growing a very successful construction business. He started out laying driveways and pavements by hand and is, without doubt, the strongest guy I've ever spent any time with. I should have had the conversation about how he might feel if I started to flake out with any physical limitations.

Woolley lives far away from Neil and I, and I often wondered what was going on in his head. Did he feel unsupported because the tyranny of distance meant he couldn't train with us regularly? Did he feel part of the team, or did he feel he wasn't important. And perhaps, more importantly, how was his training going, was he doing enough?

There was no doubt that I had fears about my own physical ability, but I know that it would have to be a most extraordinary situation for me to ever quit, particularly if my self-esteem was being put to the test. I worried, though, that I just didn't know how far the ocean would push me.

Leadership Wisdom

Share details that may have an impact on the team. Create a safe space for the exchange of views and opinions.

Looking back now and reflecting, I wish I'd had these conversations with Neil and Woolley. It would have helped me and I'm sure it would have created a safe space for them to voice the doubts and fears that they were surely experiencing.

CHAPTER 15
MY FAMILY AND WHAT I DID TO THEM

I put them through hell everyday worrying about whether I'd make it home. It's just plain selfish, rowing an ocean; I know I was a stubborn, selfish person for doing it, but more than that, I am ashamed to admit, I never really wanted to listen to my family telling me they didn't want me to do it. And, until I got home again, I didn't realise the magnitude of what they'd had to suffer throughout my absence.

My son, Joseph, was the most reluctant and asked me "What happens if you don't come back?" There was serious emotion in every syllable. I just smiled, and said "don't worry about that one, son, it'll take a lot more than that to stop me."

It was a glib, clichéd answer, I knew it at the time but it was what I said. Now that I've had time to reflect on it, I realise how selfish it was. I didn't want to hear the question, I didn't want to think about that possibility, but more than that, I didn't want anything to stop me doing what I wanted to do.

As the time grew closer to leaving, Joseph was the one person I trusted to put together my music playlist on my phone. He was not keen to let me go, but I knew he was the right person to choose exactly the music I would need to listen to, alone and lonely without them.

I mentioned earlier that Sam had flown over to see the start of the race with Neil's wife, Madeleine. It sounds horrible, but I didn't know what to say when she knocked on my door. It was a huge surprise, and it was amazing to see her, but it was heart-breaking to see what I'd put her through. As always, she looked beautiful, but I could see the strain on her face, the fear and lone-liness already in her eyes, even though she did her best to hide it from me. Despite all of this, I remained quiet because it hit me that I was leaving everything in the world that I knew and loved. It forced me to acknowledge that I was about to step into a tiny boat and row 3000 miles across the ocean. What in all hell was I thinking? I had no answer and more than that, I had no real idea what to expect.

The first night was truly horrible when it really hit me that this would be it for at least six weeks. I played Joseph's playlist as the sun went down. The first track was *How Do I Say Goodbye* by Dean Lewis and that was it, if I'd felt low before, this side-swiped me emotionally.

When my rowing shift was over I hardly slept, overcome with doubt that I could do this and overwhelmed by a longing to be safe at home while filled with a deep sadness at what I knew they'd be feeling.

Simply, I was just missing my family and wondered what the hell I was doing here, on a boat, in the middle of nowhere.

CHAPTER 16
MOTIVATION AND RESILIENCE

E ven whilst training on short early-morning rows, I was thinking to myself that it was going to be incredibly tough and I wasn't sure that I was up to it. By the time the tiny doubting voice had become a fucking loud hailer in my head, we'd cemented our team, people had started believing in us, giving us sponsorship and asking us to give motivating talks.

Our fundraising was up and running, and everything was at that stage where there would be no way I could live with the shame and embarrassment of not going through with it.

I know that when I need to motivate myself to do something, I tell people I'm going to do it. I simply change the narrative from: *I'm thinking about it* to *I'm going to do it.*

One of the guys from a pairs team that were due to row a year after us, found they just couldn't step into the boat and dropped out. I understand that totally. When you train, when you plan and prepare for such a huge challenge, it's quite abstract in a lot of ways. There's so much to do from a practical perspective and it's easy to divert yourself by locking into the tasks that need to be completed.

The actuality, the clarity of what's about to happen, only starts to hit you the night before, and then your emotions are really unleashed as you wait to cast off.

Leadership Wisdom

Be generous with praise for team members. Let them understand how much you value their contribution.

Fortunately for me, I got to train and engage in many of the preparation and fundraising talks and appearances with Neil. He was steadfast in his resolve and was loving it. I don't think I ever told him how much inspiration that gave me, and he's too modest to even think that it was possible. Training with him, attending the navigation and safety workshops, made me understand that taking on the leadership role was reasonable and that those annoying thoughts that gave me a lot of self-doubt could be silenced if I focused on the work and actually putting what I knew into practice.

I saw Neil put his anger, frustration and irritation into his rowing, which taught me to channel my own feelings into my rowing. It was pointless to fight the drudgery of it, stroke after stroke after stroke. So, I learned to put that energy into each stroke to soak up feelings I couldn't or didn't want to deal with.

LEADERSHIP NEEDS ME TO BE THE BEST VERSION OF ME

When we returned, the world was different, and it seemed like I'd been away for years. Everything seemed unreal and as though I'd forgotten the rules of civilisation. We'd been away for seven weeks, the three of us alone in the middle of nowhere, our only means of getting home, rowing. It gives you pause for thought, a lot. Being cut off from the constant noise of social media and the very connectedness of having a mobile in your pocket every waking minute and by your bedside every sleeping one, was unsettling. It emphasised how alone we were. The world was turning, just without us. Teams were winning tournaments, people were living and dying, and we didn't know anything about it. There was a lightness and simplicity about it but also a darkness that threatened to overwhelm me.

At one point we realised there was a lot of water, about two inches in one of the cabins. Everything was wet through and smelled of damp and mildew. I had thought it was just the effect of heat, accumulation of wet clothes, but two inches was too much to be attributed to that. With a rising feeling of panic, I wondered about what would happen if the boat accumulated more water. Would it be the end for us? No doubt about it. I knew that our boat was designed, like the Titanic, in sealed sections. This meant that one section could fill with water but not leak into other areas to cause catastrophic damage.

We cleared out the cabin, damp clothes and belongings everywhere, but there didn't seem to be a leak we were sure about. So, after scrubbing and drying everything as best we could, we all just hoped for the best. I still have nightmares about it now. I dream that I can't find the hole that continues to leak and then we're under water, I wake abruptly and can feel the boat's movement, even though I'm safe at home in bed next to my sleeping wife. And yes, I know, psychologists would have a lot of fun deciphering that one!

THE THINGS I'M STILL LEARNING MORE THAN A YEAR AFTER COMING HOME

I know for certain, that I will never stop learning about every minute and everything I felt during the Atlantic row. I have fulfilled a lot of speaking engagements talking about specific parts of it and how the experiences have informed my feelings about business, life, and my place in the world generally.

Soon after returning, I was asked to go on Sam Thomas's Podcast, *Everyone has a story to tell*. I thought I'd just chat about the Atlantic row and throw in a few business anecdotes, and I felt confident it would be easy. Based on my love of rugby and its discipline, I've always been interested in the parallels between training for sports and training for business. Training for the row, unexpectedly, mirrored much of what I recommend for the businesses I advise. I expected to focus on this aspect, which I think is very important and could certainly fill a podcast or two, though what happened was entirely different.

Sam Thomas is a skilled interviewer and was thoroughly prepared. He knew exactly what to ask to make me touch on feelings, thoughts and observations I never thought I'd be talking about in public. Consequently, I found myself opening up about more personal thoughts than I'd originally intended.

Since returning, I'd found it quite unsettling trying to ease back into my life, my work and my place in my family. Three months is a long time to be gone and I hadn't really considered that it wasn't just me who would change and grow, everyone else would too. It was immediately obvious that during my prolonged absence roles had developed and changed, responsibilities had adjusted and, at first, I didn't know where I fit in.

Absence may make the heart grow fonder, but it also makes returning fraught with unexpected difficulties. Being back home again, life appeared to be rolling along just as it had been, but it wasn't. I knew *I'd* be different after my adventure, the hardships, the deprivation, the physical toll, but I realised how much I had focussed on myself and what I needed, pushing everyone else's needs aside. Had I expected them to be in some kind of stasis, waiting for me to pick them up where I'd left them?

The realisation that I'd expected them to support my pursuit of achievement during the three years of training, the final preparation and the actual row hit me hard with the utter selfishness of my behaviour. When I wasn't absent, I had been preoccupied with this whole other side of my life. They had all supported me, but it was mine alone. I wasn't doing it to advance our family, I was doing it because I wanted to. I wondered how long it would take to make it up to them, if I ever could.

I spoke about the camaraderie on the boat, our team spirit, and how it was an essential part of our success. I said how important it had become to me to lead a simpler life. I think it's crucial in life and in business to help us make better decisions.

During the row, I had plenty of space to think as I wasn't being bombarded by social media, a ringing phone, questions, the important, the urgent and the downright nonsense that fills every 24 hours, and I was determined to hang onto the peace that came with less intrusion, deciding what was important to me.

My goal had become to make my life less complicated. I want it to be more enjoyable, not just for me, but for my wife, my son and my daughter.

I had thought about some of the simple things I'd started doing to uncomplicate my life and begin the work of being the best version of myself:

1. Declutter my stuff, get rid of things I didn't need.
2. Give a lot of my clothes to the charity shop, because who I am matters, not what I wear.
3. Choose more carefully the people I want to associate with because time is so precious.

4. Understand what's important to me and what's important to my family, and make better choices regarding how to spend my time and spend much more of it with them.
5. Keep working to be a better person every day.

I want to be comfortable in my own skin and not need external validation. I want to be at peace with myself, knowing that I have been able to taste, touch, smell, see and hear as much as I can in life without causing pain to others.

At the end of the podcast, Sam asked what success means to me and that was easy; it doesn't mean being rich. It means giving more than I take and being the best version of me that I can be.

CHAPTER 17
MY JOURNEY INTO LEADERSHIP AND WHAT IT MEANS TO ME

My magic bullet was the moment I realised that, as a fully grown adult and business owner, I could learn and study, and that knowledge would set me free, not trap me like I'd felt it would at school. I do what I do because I still find it shocking that most amateur sports teams are better run than a lot of businesses.

There are many reasons, or in some cases excuses, for this, but the first and really obvious one is that every sports team has a coach to train them to compete and win whereas many businesses fail to even consider training or coaching their teams for success an important part of leadership.

Whatever the activity, work or play, swimming the Channel, rowing the Atlantic or growing a business, all teams need adequate leadership and training in the specifics of their activity, whether a company or sports team.

Good training, practice and confidence is vital. Business growth cannot be achieved with employees who are 'winging it' in front of potential customers, who deserve to have a seamless and expert interaction. If the basic training is inadequate, a team will sink instead of swim.

I think I've probably heard all the excuses under the sun as to why training is not possible; the business can't afford the cost and time for good onboarding, regular training is prohibitive and unnecessary. I've heard these from a lot of businesses, particularly those that are already not achieving their potential.

It's important to realise that the cost of not preparing a workforce is far greater, including:

- Lost productivity
- Lost reputation
- Lost customers
- Constant staff turnover

Every business needs winning teams, and the only way to ensure that happens is to continue training to keep up with a competitive business environment and fast changing ways of doing business.

This is exactly the same way all sports teams are trained to compete and win before every match. Good leadership, whether it's a temporary coach or additional training for management, will pay dividends in sustainable, improved performance.

Good leaders will insist on regular training and coaching for their teams. They will use performance measures to help staff meet their potential and build proper structure into all business functions. Showing teams what best practice looks like in the business ensures they'll be able to achieve it.

THE EGO IN BEING A LEADER - CAN IT STOP YOU DOING AMAZING THINGS FOR FEAR OF FAILURE?

My answer to that is yes, very much so. After all I've learned from my life, my family, my business, my adventures, I am still not immune to my ego dictating my actions.

In 2023, Richard Carman invited me to join him and Will Manners to complete the Three Peaks Challenge in 72 hours, including cycling between the peaks. I knew I wasn't fit enough for the cycling but I did plan to complete the climbing part of the Three Peaks Challenge and then drive the support vehicle for them between each mountain.

My son, Joseph, was going to join me. Was I doing it to impress him? Mmm, perhaps not consciously, but my ego definitely was. I didn't train properly (after all, I'd just rowed the Atlantic!) and twenty minutes into the first climb, I knew I was nowhere near the level of training and fitness needed for this kind of challenge. Even worse, I was holding back Will and Rich. What could I do? How could I save face? I couldn't. I had to swallow my pride and drop out, telling them I'd instead be offering myself as their support driver. The result was incredible when they accomplished the 3 Peaks Cycle Challenge, raising over £6000 for The Brain Tumour Charity.

Leadership Wisdom

Don't let your ego stop you from being a better person.

Why did I think I could do it? I like to be out there testing myself, and I think I'm pretty good at looking at what I do, what

I want to do, and being able to assess my ability realistically. I have climbed Mont Blanc, so I know I can climb. This time? I'd totally underestimated my fitness level and knew I was going to be dead weight for Rich and Will, hampering their progress. It was a tough decision to make but my overriding feeling was not wanting to hold them back; humiliation or not.

Dropping back to 'just' one of the team was a hard lesson for me to learn. I still struggle with it, and I know I probably always will. I'm hardwired for competition and like to win. This has lessened as I've aged, but I still feel it and I know that I want to change this limiting behaviour. When you're not the one in a starring role, not leading the team, it can be tough to feel that your contribution is valuable and valued. I'm not used to taking a supporting role, but I was able to accept this was a rich experience and I'm more than grateful that they trusted Joseph and I to be the ones they'd rely on in an emergency.

LEADERSHIP ROLES APPEAR EVERYWHERE, WE CAN ALL LEAD BY EXAMPLE

Leadership roles are varied, and the term 'leader' implies one person per team. I haven't found that to be the case, not in business or in life. Any team of individuals has varied and significant skills, crucial to the overall success of a venture.

Recognising leadership ability, and not limiting it to the person up front, helps us value each individual contribution and understand the vital role each one plays in motivating other team members.

In cricket, for example, you have the captain. He/she is the outright leader, but there are subgroups with their own leaders; the bowling group, led by the bowler who can inspire best performances; the batting group, influenced by the batter who leads by example; the introverted personalities, led by the person whose mission is to keep the spirits up. Leaders lead, whether they're officially appointed or not.

CHAPTER 18
CHOOSING WHO YOU GET INTO BED WITH

Business partners are a minefield in themselves, and that's before you even get the business part. I freely admit that I go far too much by instinct and trust rather than due diligence. I think I'm getting better, but I certainly wouldn't put my money on it!

I want to believe people are good and I have been lucky a lot of the time in my journey so far. My first real business boss and then business partner, Mel, was the best. He was a mentor to me, allowed me to take the lead and was never aggressive. He was an excellent partner, almost fatherly in his care and support. This experience helped me to think that I was a good judge of character and that it would be obvious to me if someone was not quite as they seemed.

My next foray into partnership was when I merged the software business I'd bought from Mel with another supplier of the same accountancy software. As the partnership developed, there were a few surprises with the three Directors of the merged company, but we managed well and even during the financial downturn in 2008, we continued to grow. Eventually, in 2012, we were bought out at a healthy profit for us all.

Leadership Wisdom

Due diligence is essential to safeguard your team and your business from expensive mistakes.

Looking back on this now, I can see I was lucky rather than smart. I hadn't yet learned how expensive a mistake can be if you choose the wrong partner.

This happened a few years later after I had developed and grown a successful consultancy company. By now I had about twenty Associates across the UK and Australia, as well as doing consultancy work myself. As I've mentioned before, I'm always happier working in a team, and so I decided to appoint an MD to manage the team of Associates as well as having someone of equal standing to drive the business forward.

The person I selected had been working as an Associate, and would continue to do so, but with additional responsibilities. I felt that I knew him, and in exchange for his step up to management, he would receive quarterly percentage bonuses.

Whatever the reason might be, it didn't work out. He didn't really do the work and we limped on, with me shelling out money, until I decided to end the Partnership and after a few uncomfortable discussions, I had to pay him out.

My reaction to this was to batten down the hatches and do everything myself, but this was self-punishment because I had no team!

I have employed specialists, contractors and part timers but have found the most successful partnerships have come when I work with people who have skin in the game. I think this is essential and remains true with both business and an adventure like rowing the Atlantic.

During our team's first iteration entering *The World's Toughest Row*, we were a foursome. Three years preparation and training followed by a possible three months away from work, home and family is a hard ask. One team member said he'd do it but failed to contribute any funding, and because I was keen to row as a four, I accepted that his commitment to the team would be good enough. It wasn't. Without any skin in the game, he had nothing to lose by joining us at first and then leaving. This was a blow to the three of us who remained, and we needed permission to change our entry to a threesome, and our boat built for four, would now be rowed by three, with all the additional weight now placed on our shoulders (literally).

Leadership Wisdom

Business partners need to have skin in the game to ensure they are as committed to the success of the venture as you are.

I hope that I have grown, if not better, then more straightforward and upfront about joint opportunities. Since the row, my priorities have changed a lot. I was in discussion with two potential business partners for more than four months before deciding to pull the pin. Now I'm in a new and exciting business venture with four others, and we all have skin in the game. I am finding it invigorating and I don't have the same level of anxiety that I've felt in the past. It's proper teamwork, we're all very different and bring unique skills to the table but are all very committed to our vision and what success looks like.

Have I learned my lesson? At this juncture, I would say, of course. But, my default is to trust people, because I like to trust people and I want the world to be a place where good exists, so I won't rule out the possibility that I'll take a chance on someone again, relying only on my gut instinct!

CHAPTER 19
RECAPPING THE IMPORTANT LESSONS, I'VE LEARNED IN MY JOURNEY SO FAR

Recognising leadership motivates people and gives them responsibility to continue to perform and lead others to greater achievements. When you're 'seen' you do better and when your leadership is recognised, even in a minor role, it makes you feel great.

Understanding that wanting to climb the peaks was my ego talking, but knowing how vital the support vehicle was to Rich and Will, allowed me to forget about my ego. I enjoyed every second of the trip and the time I spent with Joseph. It was a priceless gift.

I've never made a secret about leaving school at 16, formal education just didn't do it for my teenage self. I wanted rugby, I wanted fishing, I wanted real life.

Joining a trawler boat as the tea boy, and gutting and washing fish was definitely real life. It didn't take me long to realise that what I wanted for myself was not only out of reach, but it had also never felt so far away. I didn't recognise how much it was teaching me about life, leadership, and teamwork; lessons I've never forgotten, lessons that I value to this day.

We all have a definition of a good leader and there isn't a one size fits all answer because everybody's very different. You might feel you have natural leadership ability and take it easily in your stride or you might struggle with it every day, worrying you're not good enough. Whatever you feel about your leadership ability actually doesn't matter, it's about being authentic and recognising the value of everyone in the team. People decide whether or not they want to follow you and it really is this simple; if people are following you, you're a leader.

Leadership Wisdom

Good leaders recognise they must work with their team to earn their respect, not their friendship.

I know I am now a confident leader, but I am most definitely still on my leadership journey. I remember every day what it felt like to have a good leader and what I responded to. Leaders need to influence their teams and show what needs to be done. This involves emotional intelligence, really seeing the different personalities and being able to communicate effectively with each person.

I recognised early that success isn't only about knowledge or position, it's about being consistent and continuing to grow as you apply your knowledge. As a leader, I am careful to make it clear what my definition of success is and how I want to achieve it. I am open to the thoughts and ideas of the team and like to have collaboration and innovations from them.

Controlling my own destiny means having the courage to face issues and challenges, and not being afraid to be vulnerable and ask for help when I need it. I have always valued leaders who show me that I am valued for my contribution.

I aim to lead with a light hand, trusting the skills and ability of my team and resisting the urge to micromanage, but I know I am not always successful in this. Practice makes perfect and I continue to keep trying.

I have learned the hard way that being swift in making tough decisions is by far the best way for all concerned. After considering all the options, and making sure that everything possible has been done, a timely decision saves a huge amount of difficulty, destabilisation and heartache.

Learning how to communicate effectively with all the key stakeholders; the team, the Board, Senior Management and customers, is vital to good leadership and success.

Leadership Wisdom

Great leaders understand that the journey will never end, there are always so many ways to be better.

When I start to feel I'm getting the hang of it, I know I must keep going. I aim never to think I've got to the best I can be. I want to continue to learn and continue to improve. I won't ever get to the end of my journey into leadership.

I want to feel confident even when I'm feeling self-doubt. I remember on the row, how sharing my vulnerability was not a sign of weakness but brought the team closer together.

Admitting I'm wrong or don't know something is still confronting but I do it. I know that honesty and authenticity help the team succeed.

We all have a definition of a good leader and there isn't a one-size-fits-all answer because we're all very different. You might have natural leadership ability and take it easily in your stride, or you might struggle with it every day.

Leadership Wisdom

Leading by example gives you the opportunity to spread a positive message and make a difference.

There's no right or wrong way to go about the business of leadership. It can be complex, rewarding, thankless, frustrating and impossible but when your team starts to be consistently successful, and you realise that you're no longer flying by the seat of your pants, you can start to enjoy it.

Ultimately, enjoying being a leader is the thing that matters. Confidence and enjoyment are so important to living a happy life spreading good into the world. Leading by example is never more important than when you are spreading a positive message and making a difference wherever you go.

MY THOUGHTS ABOUT WISDOM AS A LEADER

I don't think imposter syndrome ever goes away, I've just learned different techniques to overcome it and power through. I believe in keeping my friends close and making absolutely **NO ENEMIES**. It makes no sense to me. There will always be disagreements, especially in an increasingly divisive society, but enemies? No, it's never necessary.

I continually strive to be quick to recognise my strengths and weaknesses, and not be ashamed or too proud to admit them.

When leading a team, I think it's very important to know what you're capable of and to let the team know too. This way, your team have the opportunity to understand and pick up any slack for you.

The same principle applies when building a strong family base. Sharing responsibility with everyone able to play to their strengths creates a strong family team who know how to pull together, which is especially important considering the age range in a typical family and the unique challenges that brings.

My adventures have taught me so much and influenced how I act with work colleagues. The pressure of putting myself in extreme circumstances has helped me have a more logical perspective on solving business challenges. Interestingly, I found myself applying some of my business methodology to manage different tasks to ensure our Atlantic row kept to schedule and got us safely home.

Leadership Wisdom

A good leader is the first to say: how can I help?

On the boat, if I felt one of us was struggling, my first thought was *how can I help?* Since I've been back and immersed in the business environment, I have realised how important that thought is. It doesn't matter if it's a team difficulty, a CEO or MD, the words "how can I help?" are the key to solving problems. Encouraging candour helps get to the heart of what needs to be fixed.

Leadership Wisdom

A good leader is sympathetic to how differently individuals may see the world and doesn't enforce a one-rule-fits-all policy.

My goal is to inspire, to help people think differently, to accept what they're working with, obstacles, disadvantages, commitments and find ways to work with these to achieve balance and clarity.

With age comes knowledge and a greater understanding of how much leadership matters. When we pick leaders based on inauthentic media driven ideology, we are endangering what we want to achieve.

I think that by now we all understand the dangers and misuse of social media and how damaging it can be. We do need to use it responsibly and learn to live in the real world with authentic values to lessen the impact of what we see. I think about it a lot and try to practice mindful use, and encourage thoughtful and calm practice, particularly in my own family. I also understand the huge impact of peer pressure and how difficult it is to manage this when every minute of our day is documented online.

I know that I will always work to be the best version of me that I can be. Who judges? I do. I simply aim to be better tomorrow than I am today. Always learning, always improving. I know there will always be someone faster, stronger, smarter, younger, louder, more confident and I know it doesn't matter. I don't have to be in competition with other people. Only what I do matters because that's all I can control. And I won't ever be afraid to hit the pause button if I'm feeling anxious, because I know how important good mental practice is. I can only be of value to my family and friends if I keep myself strong and lead by example.

WHY EXTREME ADVENTURES?

Because it helps me. Testing myself, putting myself at the edge of endurance and ability. Devising a strategy for success, training, and preparation. Leading a team of people, wildly different from myself but with the same goal. Learning about myself the hard way, when I'm under pressure, and when I have to endure hardship. I understand how easy my life is. How conventional, what a privileged position I have in the scheme of things. I don't ever want to forget that or take it for granted.

Extreme adventures may seem self-indulgent to some but for me, they wake me up. They force me to take a cold, hard look at the difficulties in the world and make me want to use my influence, small as it is, to do better, reach more people and help bring about positive change.

Different things work for different people so I urge everyone to find what works for them. The thing that makes you feel good about yourself and fits your life. It might be golf, cooking, therapy, running, rugby, cycling, gardening, knitting, puzzles, sailing, reading, singing, painting, making music, the list of possibilities is endless. Talk to your friends, experience different things, try stuff out, try everything, join things and be fearless in your search. And always be kind, be there for people, but mostly be there for yourself – like on a plane, put on your own oxygen mask before helping others, help yourself to be the best and then lead by example.

CHAPTER 20
AND NOW?

W here do I fit in? I still don't know, and that's OK because it's the journey that matters and every day, I learn something new.

It might be about leadership, or it might be about being a better person. Every time I speak to a different group of people, business groups, clients, schools, there's an exchange of ideas, and even if I'm there to motivate or teach something specific, I always come away with new insights.

I'm becoming more and more aware of unconscious bias and how easy it is to assume we know a person based on all sorts of preconceptions. This is an area that I am working hard to address in my mentor sessions and motivational speaking.

Travelling to other countries and seeing the huge variety of life, cultures and living styles is truly enlightening. It also reinforces my understanding that as a person in a privileged position, it is up to me to do my bit to lead the way in my sphere of influence, to make equality not just a far distant dream, but a reality.

There have been, and I'm sure will always be, days when the journey seems unbearably hard, but I am learning to love every part of it. And the hard days are often the most valuable learning opportunities. I do spend a lot of time reflecting on my past mistakes, probably too much, trying to learn from them to make better decisions in the future. I am very aware of the danger in spending too long thinking about them and getting caught in a loop that erodes my confidence. I'm getting better at not regretting past mistakes, but acknowledging them, learning from them, and moving on. I know that I came late to enjoying and embracing the search for knowledge after rejecting it so wholeheartedly at school.

I'm very pleased to have found a new enthusiasm for learning and an understanding that it's a lifelong adventure. I get to choose what and how I learn, I'm not limited to a narrow school curriculum. Everything and anything is available to me. I can and do learn about very different areas of life, following up on all kinds of random things I hear about.

I feel confident that it's possible to learn anything if it interests you. A good example came from the preparations for the row when I managed all the instruments and technical equipment. Neil and Woolley didn't really know how to use them, not because they were too complex or beyond them, but they simply had little interest, and they trusted me. Why was it easy for me? Because I wanted to learn.

I think being a good leader means having a quality we recognise but can't quite describe. It encompasses confidence and enjoyment, it means embracing all the difficult times, the joyful times, the hard work, the frustrations, the failures, the times when nothing at all seems to work until it does. It means enjoying all of that and doing it again and again, because that's what a good leader has signed up for and I wouldn't have it any other way.

I'm very happy to be a person with a question mark over them, not able to be labelled as this, that or the other.

I have an appetite for the diversity of life, and I want to have the freedom to be outside of any box with a label saying *Matt Garman belongs here*.

I say this not because I think I'm better than anyone else, but because it would mean that I have stopped looking, stopped learning, and there's so much more to see, to try and to do.

I'm on a journey, its unconventional, I know, and it's not over yet…

9 781838 329990